The Drummer's Bible

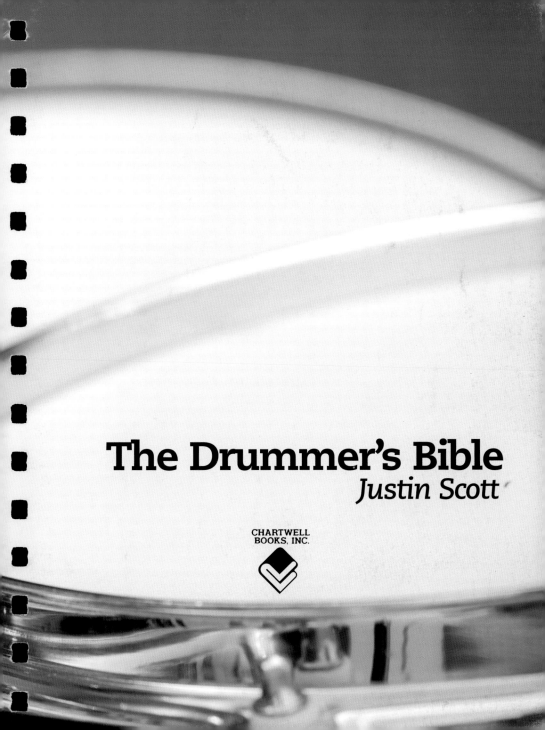

The Drummer's Bible
Justin Scott

CHARTWELL
BOOKS, INC.

A QUARTO BOOK

Published in 2008 by
Chartwell Books, Inc.
A division of Book Sales, Inc.
114 Northfield Avenue
Edison, New Jersey 08837
USA

ISBN-13: 978-0-7858-2364-3
ISBN-10: 0-7858-2364-6
QUAR.PDR

This book was designed
and produced by
Quarto Inc.
The Old Brewery
6 Blundell Street
London N7 9BH

Project Editor Ben Hubbard
Assistant Editor Emma Poulter
Designer Ben Dakin
Photographer Martin Norris
Illustrator Kuo Kang Chen
Sound Engineer Pete Riley
Art Director Caroline Guest

Creative Director Moira Clinch
Publisher Paul Carslake

Printed by Midas Printing Int'l
Ltd., China
Color separation by Modern Age
Repro House Ltd., Hong Kong

Contents

PART 3: THE LESSONS

contents

About this book

This book provides the beginner with all of the essential information needed to start playing the drums quickly, and with a minimum of fuss.

The Drummer's Bible is organized into sections that follow each other in a chronological sequence. But these sections have also been designed to "stand alone," allowing the reader to dip in-and-out of any section of the book as they please. This enables the learner to tailor their course of study to their own specific interests. However the book is read—in the traditional way, from beginning to end, or in a more random sequence—every section is individually designed to get the learner onto the drumset and playing it.

The chapters at the beginning of the book provide an introduction to the drumset, giving tips and advice on choosing the right drums, tuning them, and setting them up in the correct way. Next, there's an introduction to reading music and understanding musical notation. The middle of the book concerns itself with actual drumming lessons, concentrating on: technique, coordination, vocabulary, and reading. These lessons are introduced in a progressive, non-threatening way and are designed to teach the beginner actual grooves they can play on a drumset. The end of the book focuses on some of the most exciting styles of drumming played in modern music.

Learning to read music can be a daunting task for any beginner musician. This book's approach is to take the confusion out of learning to read drumming music by presenting the information both visually and aurally. The traditional notation provided in the musical exercises is supplemented with easy-to-understand diagrams and icons, which walk you through every stage of learning a new groove. The accompanying CD contains audio examples of many of the exercises, so you can listen to a musical exercise and read it at the same time.

All of this is presented in a handy and compact spiral-bound format, that not only means this book is easily transported in a stick bag, but also that it opens out flat, enabling it to rest conveniently on any music stand.

So now all you need to do is grab your sticks and start learning.

Justin Scott

Turn the page for an explanation of the symbols used in the book.

About the exercises in this book

To help you get the most out of the exercises in this book, look at these two pages. They explain the different graphics, diagrams, and icons that will enable you to understand each exercise more easily, and consequently transfer the music from the page to the drums quickly and effectively.

Understanding the graphic diagrams used in the coordination section

To reinforce the musical notation, many of the exercises are accompanied by graphic diagrams that use special icons to represent drums and cymbals. These icons are arranged on a matrix underneath the notation, making it easy to see on which count each drum or cymbal is played, as well as how they line up with one another. In these diagrams, the following icons are used:

⬯   Closed hi-hat

⬯   Open hi-hat

⬯   Ride cymbal

▢   Snare drum

▯   Bass drum

These are arranged on a grid or matrix as in the example below.

Want to read music?

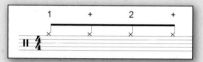

A guide to the musical notation conventions used throughout this book can be found in the Reading and Notation section on page 38.

The matrix

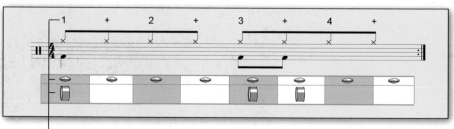

The shaded column denotes the beat, and here the notation indicates that on the first beat you play the hi-hat and bass drum simultaneously.

Understanding the "motion" diagrams

To help you understand which drums are being used in the vocabulary exercises (pages 217–233), special diagrams called motion diagrams are used. These depict a standard five-piece drumset as seen from above, and feature numbers that show the order in which the individual drums are to be played. The fifth drum is the one played with the foot (bass drum) underneath drums 2 and 3.

1: Snare drum
2. High tom
3. Mid tom
4. Floor tom
5. Bass drum

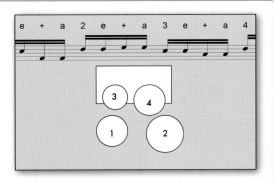

The CD

You will find the accompanying CD an invaluable tool in working through this book, as it contains many of the key musical exercises actually being played. All of the exercises that can be heard on the CD are denoted with the relevant track number.

Fold-out flap

Opposite page 256, you'll find a useful fold-out flap with a key to the abbreviations and notations used throughout this book. Keep it open at all times, until you become familiar with how the material is presented.

A note for left-handed drummers

All of the exercises in this book are presented for right-handed drummers. In the coordination matrix right, it indicates that the ride cymbal is to be played with the right hand (RH)—a left-handed drummer would simply use the left hand instead, which would be denoted as LH. Similarly, where specific stickings are indicated, for example R L R R L R L L, the left-handed drummer would "invert" the sticking and play L R L L R L R R.

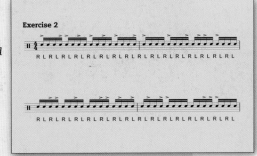

Part 1:
The drumset

A Brief History of the Drumset

In the late nineteenth century, New Orleans was a melting pot of different cultures. French, Spanish, English, and German migrants brought with them European musical traditions, which included their love of military music.

African slaves that were transported to the city brought different musical traditions, which often featured sophisticated rhythmic elements. Also, at the end of the American Civil War, the pawnshops of New Orleans were inundated with military snare and bass drums. Consequently, almost every civic, social, and religious event that took place in New Orleans involved a marching band. The same bands would also feature at night, in the many dance halls of Storyville, the city's red light district.

Second-line musicians marching through the streets of New Orleans.

1895	1899	1910		1920
Dee Dee Chandler builds the first bass drum pedal.	*U.G. Leedy introduces the first snare drum stand.*	*William F. Ludwig introduces his new bass drum pedal.*	*The "traps" sets evolve, as drummers start to add various percussion instruments to their set-ups.*	*The Walberg and Auge company introduce the first "lowboy" stand.*

A Fife player accompanied by a snare drum and bass drum.

The bass drum pedal

In 1895, a drummer called Dee Dee Chandler built a homemade device that enabled him to play the bass drum with his foot. Unlike the modern design, it was not particularly effective. However, Chandler had created the first bass drum pedal, and from this innovation came the genesis of the modern American drumset.

In 1909, William F. Ludwig built a new bass drum pedal that offered greater speed and control than any of its predecessors. Ludwig's wooden prototypes were very popular, and by teaming up with his engineer brother-in-law, Ludwig started manufacturing the pedals in cast metal. This Ludwig design still endures today.

Double drumming

Indoors, the bands were not marching, so it became possible for a single drummer to play both the snare and bass drum at the same time. This was achieved by having the bass drum set up at an angle to the right of the snare drum, so it could be played with sticks. This practice became known as "double drumming."

Ludwig "Speed King" pedal.

1930	1936		
Companies Leedy, Slingerland, and Ludwig begin to feature hi-hat stands in their catalogues.	Slingerland design the first tunable tom toms in response to a request by Gene Krupa, drummer with Benny Goodman's band.	Chicago drummer, Dave Tough, who played with Woody Herman's band, begins experimenting with larger cymbals, and the ride cymbal is born.	Innovation all but stops due to the war.

A Brief History of the Drumset

Further developments

It was not long before drummers sought to expand their sonic palette, and various new percussion instruments were added to the drumming ensemble. Chinese immigrants coming to America's west coast brought with them a rich musical culture, and a plethora of new and interesting instruments, such as temple blocks, which were arranged in sets across the bass drum.

The Chinese introduced the "Pieng Ku"—the brightly painted precursors to modern tom toms. Pieng Ku were about 10–15 inches in diameter and three inches deep, and were mounted on the bass drum.

Chinese cymbals with their distinctive look, and "trashy" sound were also incorporated. These cymbals were either spring-mounted on top of the bass drum, where they could be struck

Drumming great, Chick Webb at his traps set.

with a stick; or, on the bass drum hoop, where they were played with a specially modified two-beater bass drum pedal. Later, Turkish cymbals were added. The name given to this mish-mash of percussive paraphernalia was "traps."

1950	1960	1970
Marion "Chick" Evans invents the synthetic drumhead but the Remo company, founded by Remo Belli, makes it commercially popular.	The Rogers company lead the way in improving drum hardware through their Swiv-O-Matic series.	Improvements in hardware manufacturing make it possible to have larger, multi-tom set-ups, often incorporating single-headed concert toms.

The hi-hat

Around this time, a device called a snowshoe was incorporated into the ever-evolving drumset. This was a spring-hinged footplate, between which two cymbals were mounted. Playing it with the left foot, the drummer was able to get a short, staccato "chick" sound, or a longer "splash" sound.

The lowboy, pictured here, was introduced in the 1920s.

Modern hi-hat pedal manufactured by Mapex.

Although it introduced new possibilities to the drumset, the snowshoe did not lend itself to speed or rhythmic accuracy, and it was not long before a number of alternatives were offered. The most popular of these was the "lowboy," which resembled the modern hi-hat used today. The main difference was its height of 10 inches, which allowed it to accommodate larger cymbals. Finally, the cymbals were raised so they could be played with sticks. This was the blueprint for the modern hi-hat stand that is so familiar to us today.

By the late 1930s, manufacturers offered complete drumsets. The use of traps declined, large military bass drums and deep snare drums were no longer fashionable, and smaller drums became popular. Later, innovations such as tunable tom toms, larger cymbals, improved hardware, and synthetic drumheads made drums easier to play. Today, there are hundreds of manufacturers worldwide, offering an amazing array of drums, cymbals, drumsticks, drumheads, cases, and accessories.

	1980		
Japanese companies enter the marketplace offering high quality drums and heavy-duty hardware.	Electronic percussion begins with devices like the Syndrum.	Manufacturing standards continue to improve and many new drum companies appear. Deeper drums called power sizes become fashionable.	Drum Workshop introduce the first practical double pedal.

Anatomy of a Drumset

The drumsets played today evolved through a combination of diverse percussion instruments, taken from different musical cultures, and technical innovation.

Drumsets come in a wide variety of sizes and configurations, depending on the style of music being played, and are produced all over the world by numerous manufacturers. This chapter will explore the various components of the modern drumset, as well as looking at some of the different configurations used in different types of music

Crash cymbal

A standard 5-piece Mapex acoustic drumset.

Crash cymbal

Ride cymbal

Tom toms

Hi-hat

Cymbal stands

Bass drum

High tom

Mid tom

Snare drum

Floor tom

Hi-hat stand

Hi-hat pedal

Bass drum pedal

Drum stool

The same 5-piece Mapex acoustic drumset, shown from the back.

This drumset with its single-rack tom and large bass drum was favored by 1960s Rock drummers.

This double bass drum setup with its numerous toms is typically used by Heavy metal drummers.

Anatomy of a Drum

Now that you are familiar with the various components of the modern drumset, and the common configurations used to play different styles of music, the next stage is to explore what goes into making an individual drum.

While all drums in the set are basically comprised of the same components, the drum featured in the example opposite is a snare drum. This is because the snare drum has a number of additional design features not seen on bass drums or toms.

Shell

Bass drums and toms are traditionally made from wooden shells, and snare drum shells from both metal and wood. Maple and birch are the most common woods used in the construction of high-end drums, and, at the lower end of the market, less expensive woods such as basswood are often used. Metal-shelled snare drums are commonly made from steel or brass, but copper, bronze and aluminum are also used.

Some manufacturers have experimented with less conventional drum materials. In the 1970s, clear acrylic drums, like Ludwig's Vistalite line, became popular. More recently, drums have been made from exotic woods, chosen for their interesting sonic characteristics and unique appearance.

Wooden shells are commonly made up from a number of plies bent into a cylindrical shape, although solid one-piece shells and shells made from blocks of wood are now popular. Metal shells are either cast, or made from

This photo of a snare drum has been "deconstructed" on the opposite page to illustrate how it is pieced together.

a single sheet of metal rolled into a cylinder. A good shell should be as close to a perfect cylinder as possible.

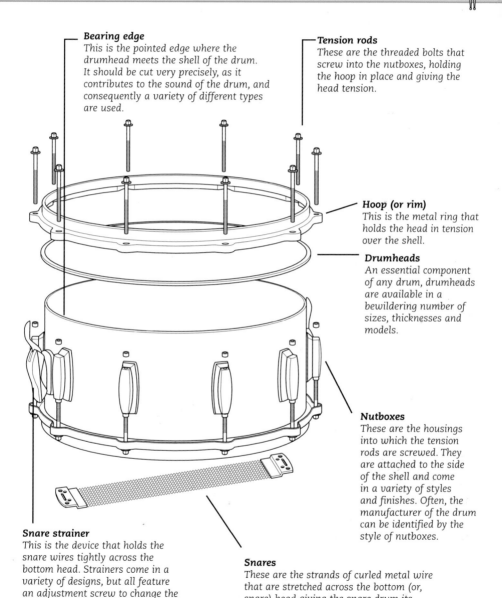

Bearing edge
This is the pointed edge where the drumhead meets the shell of the drum. It should be cut very precisely, as it contributes to the sound of the drum, and consequently a variety of different types are used.

Tension rods
These are the threaded bolts that screw into the nutboxes, holding the hoop in place and giving the head tension.

Hoop (or rim)
This is the metal ring that holds the head in tension over the shell.

Drumheads
An essential component of any drum, drumheads are available in a bewildering number of sizes, thicknesses and models.

Nutboxes
These are the housings into which the tension rods are screwed. They are attached to the side of the shell and come in a variety of styles and finishes. Often, the manufacturer of the drum can be identified by the style of nutboxes.

Snare strainer
This is the device that holds the snare wires tightly across the bottom head. Strainers come in a variety of designs, but all feature an adjustment screw to change the exact tension of the snare wires.

Snares
These are the strands of curled metal wire that are stretched across the bottom (or, snare) head giving the snare drum its characteristic "snappy" sound.

Drumheads

A new drumset will come fitted with drumheads as standard. However, at some point it will be necessary to replace them.

There are a number of reasons why you might replace drumheads with the type of heads that your set came with. Often, especially at the entry-level end of the market, manufacturers will fit kits with cheaper drumheads. High quality replacement heads will improve the sound and "tunability" of your drums. Also, the heads that come with a new set are likely to be general purpose, where a different type of head may suit your tastes more. This chapter will explore the various types of drumheads available.

Anatomy of a drumhead

Originally, drumheads were made of natural materials such as calfskin, but today they are made of synthetic materials like polyester. Such materials are more durable and resistant to changes in temperature and humidity. All heads are constructed in basically the same way—they are made from a synthetic film, set with resin into an alloy or plastic ring. Beyond this basic design they come with a variety of features, to enable a variety of different sounds.

Bullet-proof heads

In the 1970s, an American company called Duraline offered drumheads made of Kevlar, the same material that bulletproof vests are made from. These heads were so strong that they could even be played with a hole in them.

Batter heads

These heads fit on to the top of the drum, which you strike with the sticks.

Coated or clear?

Most commonly, drumheads come in one of two finishes: coated or clear. Clear heads are transparent and smooth in texture, while coated heads have a coarse white finish. This coating adds mass to the head, causing it to have a slightly lower tone, while the rough texture accentuates the attack of the stick. Coated heads can also be played with brushes.

Black or white?

While the vast majority of coated heads are manufactured with a white coating, some companies such as Aquarian produce coated heads with a more unique appearance such as their Jack DeJohnette signature models. These feature a durable black coating that gives them a very distinctive look.

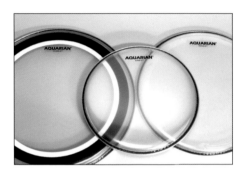

Sizes
The size of the head is determined by the size of the drum it is for. A 12-inch tom takes a 12-inch drumhead.

Thickness
The thickness of drumheads is measured in mils (1 mil equals 0.001 of an inch) although practically speaking, heads come in three weights—thin, medium, and thick. Manufacturers generally have their own names for each of these weights, however, the standard was set some time ago by Remo who labeled the weights of their heads—Diplomat, Ambassador, and Emperor respectively. In the drumhead business these names have become synonyms for thin, medium, and thick. Thinner heads are more sensitive but less durable than thicker heads. To increase the durability of some single ply heads most manufacturers offer models reinforced at the center with a dot.

Dampening rings
Some drumheads are designed to reduce or eliminate some of the resonance (or sustain), and overtones of the drum. The most common design is a built-in dampening ring around the outer edge, such as with Aquarian Focus-X drumheads. Other products are available to dampen the sound of a drum. These include O-rings and MoonGel, which are both placed externally on the head.

Single or double ply?
There is some discrepancy between the ply of different manufacturers but as a guide, thin heads are made from single ply around 7.5-mil thick, and medium heads are made from a single ply around 10-mil thick. Interestingly, thick heads are usually made from two plies of film, each around 7-mil thick.

Tuning: Some Basic Principles

Firstly, there are no hard and fast rules when it comes to tuning drums. If it sounds good then it probably is good. However, understanding a few basic principles will enable you to achieve the sound you are looking for quickly and consistently.

Fitting a new drumhead

Once you have chosen the type of head you want, the following process will help you install it correctly.

Seating the drumhead

When fitting a brand new head it's important to "seat" it first. This serves two important functions: firstly, it stretches out the head making it less likely to detune when it's first played. Secondly, it shapes the head to the bearing edge enabling it to resonate more freely and making fine-tuning easier.

1: *Start by placing the drum on a stable, level surface and unscrew all of the tension rods.*

Then, remove the hoop and the old head from the drum.

2: *Using a soft, dry cloth, wipe the bearing edge and the hoop clean, removing any dirt or dust that might have built up.*

The drum key

To remove the old head and fit and tune the new one, you will need a drum key. Pictured here, this is the small tool that enables you to loosen and tighten the tension rods. Your drum or drumset should have come with one, and so make sure you have yours to hand before proceeding.

4: *Using your fingers, turn the tension rods until they begin to tighten on the hoop.*

3: *Place the new head on the drum, and replace the hoop and tension rods.*

5: *Using your drum key, begin tightening each tension rod by turning it a half turn. To ensure even tension in the head, it is important to tighten the tension rods uniformly. To achieve this, they are tuned in a specific sequence depending on the number of lugs on the drum. Continue tightening the head until it is at a pitch higher than you want.*

Tuning: Some Basic Principles

6: *Next, press the center of the head firmly with the palm of your hand. Don't worry if the head makes some "cracking" sounds at this point. This is just excess resin breaking away from the ring and is quite normal.*

7: *Detune the head completely using the tuning sequence. Now the head has been seated, you can begin to tune the drum to its final pitch.*

8: *Start the sequence again, turning each lug a quarter turn until you reach the desired pitch.*

9: *Continue to follow the sequence, fine tuning each lug until they are at the same tension. You can ascertain this by tapping the head with the drum key at the edge close to the lug. When all lugs are at the same pitch, they are at the same tension and the head is in tune.*

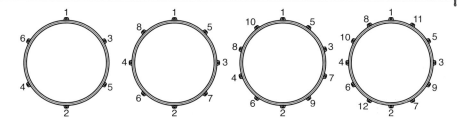

The above diagram illustrates the correct sequence to tune a 6, 8, 10, and 12 lug drum.

Head tension

Once you understand the tuning process, the tension you tune your drum to, is up to you. As a guide, higher tensions give higher pitch, brighter tone, longer sustain, and greater projection; whereas lower tensions give lower pitch, darker tone, shorter sustain, and less projection. The key is to experiment, but bear in mind that all drums have an optimum tuning range within which they will give you the best sound.

Relative tension?

The vast majority of drums have a batter head and a resonant head, but how should these be tuned to one another? Generally, a drum will have maximum volume and sustain when both heads are at the same tension, and the drum is within its optimum tuning range. The exception is the snare drum, where you should start with the batter head higher than the snare head.

A word about bass drums

Because of the size and function of the bass drum, your approach to tuning it will be different than that of the other drums. It is common to place some kind of material inside the drum before fitting the heads, in order to dampen it. Most often, a pillow is used which is large enough to touch both the batter, and resonant heads at the same time.

Once you fit the heads, it is best to tune both to the same tension. Start by tightening the batter head just tightly enough to remove any wrinkles. If at this tension the bass drum feels a little unresponsive and difficult to play, try

tuning it up slightly, until it feels better. The idea is to get a balance between a "fat" sound with lots of low end, and playability.

The resonant head on the bass drum often has a small hole in it. This does two things—firstly, it allows air to escape quickly from the drum when it's struck, significantly reducing resonance. Secondly, it enables a microphone to be placed inside the drum. It also has the advantage of making it easier to reach in and reposition any pillows that you might be using to dampen the drum.

Cymbals

Ancient cymbals date back over two thousand years, but the art of modern cymbal-making, which has Turkish origins, is only a few hundred years old.

Today, a vast number of models and sizes are available from manufacturers all over the world, and choosing the right cymbal can be a challenge.

Hi-hats

Hi-hat cymbals are sold in pairs and usually the bottom cymbal is heavier than the top. Ranging between 10" (inches), and 15" in diameter, the most popular sizes are 13", and 14". They are mounted horizontally on the hi-hat stand and can be played with the sticks or using the pedal, with the foot. The primary function of the hi-hats is to state the time.

Rides

The ride cymbal will be the largest cymbal, ranging from 18" to 22" in size, with 20" models tending to be the most popular. The function of the ride cymbal is similar to that of the hi-hat, that is, to state the time. So, as well as having a large diameter, ride cymbals are relatively thick, which gives them a more controlled sound.

A good, general-purpose cymbal set-up, can comprise a set of hi-hats, a ride cymbal, and one or two crashes. However, there are a few other cymbal types to become familiar with.

Crashes

Crashes serve a very different purpose than ride cymbals. They are generally used to accentuate certain rhythmic points within the music, and are consequently designed in a different way. They range in size from 14" to 19", and come in a variety of thicknesses depending on their chosen application. They are played with the shoulder of the stick on the edge of the cymbal, and the resulting sound is explosive—perfect for punctuating the form of a tune.

Splashes

Splashes are smaller, thinner crash cymbals, ranging from 6" to 12" in diameter. They produce a shorter, higher-pitched sound, and are generally used to expand the sonic possibilities of a basic cymbal set-up.

Effects cymbals

Effects cymbals include a range of different designs including gongs, bells, and plates, all intended to offer exotic sounding alternatives to traditional cymbals.

Chinas

Chinese cymbals have a distinctive shape and are very different than their Turkish counterparts. Ranging in size from 12" to 22", they have a unique flanged edge and a "square" bell—a design that gives them their idiosyncratic sound. They are most commonly mounted "upside down," so that the shoulder of the stick can be played on the curved part of the cymbal's edge. They can also be used as an alternative to both rides and crashes.

Anatomy of a Cymbal

The anatomy of a cymbal is important, as each of the cymbal's parts play a different role in its overall makeup. A cymbal's bell, bow, edge, weight, and diameter all add to its character, and understanding these different parts will help you choose the right cymbals for you.

Hi-hat

The hi-hat consists of two cymbals on a stand. Cymbal characteristics are similar for all cymbals: hi-hats, effects, splashes, crashes, or rides (see previous article).

Diameter
After model type, size is the most common way of classifying cymbals. When we talk about the size of a cymbal, we are referring to its diameter, which is measured in inches.

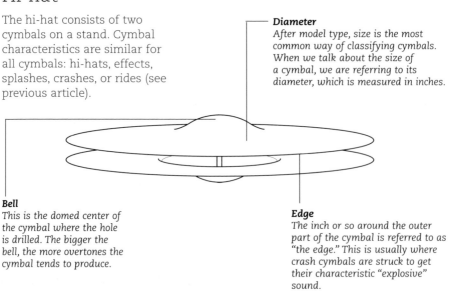

Bell
This is the domed center of the cymbal where the hole is drilled. The bigger the bell, the more overtones the cymbal tends to produce.

Edge
The inch or so around the outer part of the cymbal is referred to as "the edge." This is usually where crash cymbals are struck to get their characteristic "explosive" sound.

Profile
The higher the profile that a cymbal has, the higher in pitch it will be, and the fewer overtones it will have.

Weight
The weight of a cymbal affects the volume, articulation, and character of its sound. Usually, thinner cymbals are quieter, more responsive, and tend to have a fuller sound that is lower in pitch than heavier cymbals. Of course, thinner cymbals also tend to be less durable than heavier ones.

Bow

The bow is the curved part of the cymbal between the bell and the edge. The thickness of the bow determines the weight of the cymbal, and therefore its sound. The degree of bow curvature determines the profile of the cymbal, another important characteristic of the cymbal's sound.

Ride area

The ride area is the part of the bow roughly halfway between the bell and the edge. It is where you would play with the tip of the stick if you wanted the cymbal to function more as a ride.

Crash area

The crash area is the outer part of the bow near the edge, and would normally be played with the shoulder of the stick when the cymbal is required to function more like crash.

Ride

Here is a typical ride cymbal, clearly showing the bell, the bow, and the edge.

Drumsticks: Choosing the Right Pair

Walk into any drum store looking for drumsticks and you will find yourself confronted with an unfathomable number of options.

With so many different colors, shapes, and sizes on the market, how do you choose the right pair of sticks? Drumsticks can be viewed as a drummer's tools of the trade, and like most tools it is simply a question of selecting the most appropriate ones for the job. The next few pages will provide all of the information you will require to make that choice.

Anatomy of a stick

Butt
This is the back end of the stick and acts as a counterweight. Occasionally, a drummer might flip the stick around and play with it in reverse. This is common when playing a cross-stick, or when extra volume and power are needed for the backbeat.

Body
This is the main part of the stick and the bit that you actually grip. It is also the part of the stick that strikes the hoop of the drum when you play rimshots.

Tip
This is the part that usually strikes the drum or cymbal.

Shoulder
This is the point at which the body begins to taper toward the tip.

Stick sizes

Manufacturers use various model numbers to classify their sticks. Traditionally, a universal system involving letters and numbers was used to identify the size and recommended application of different models. Although this is still the most commonly used system, nowadays many manufacturers label sticks with names exclusive to their particular brand. An example of this is signature sticks, made to the requirements of a specific drummer, and bearing his or her name.

Within each category, the number describes the thickness (or diameter) of the body of the stick. Interestingly, the smaller the number the greater the diameter—so a 7A is actually smaller than a 5A. But because of their intended application, a 5B is bigger than a 5A.

Rock drummer Alex Valen Halen's signature sticks.

Universal model numbers

These comprise a number and a letter. For example, "5A" or, "2B." The letter describes the suggested application. Three letters are used: "S," "B," and "A."

"S" model sticks are the largest and were originally designed for street use, which includes marching bands or drum corps, where extra volume and projection are needed.

"B" model sticks were originally intended for band use, and are consequently not as big as "S" model sticks.

"A" model sticks were intended for orchestral use, where soft playing is often necessary. Consequently the sticks in this category are the smallest and lightest of all.

Tips come in a number of different shapes and sizes and have a subtle but important effect on sound and feel, especially when playing on the cymbals. The most common tips are: Round tip; Acorn tip; Bead tip; Barrel tip; Nylon tip.

Acorn tip

Barrel tip

Nylon tip

Bead tip

Drumsticks: Choosing the Right Pair

In addition to drumsticks, there are a range of other items available such as brushes, mallets, and multirods, all designed to help you get different sounds and colors from your drums and cymbals.

Brushes

Although very versatile, brushes are most commonly associated with jazz drumming. They comprise a set of plastic, or metal, bristles, which fan out from a handle that is most often made of rubber-coated metal but can also be made of plastic or wood. Some designs are telescoping, allowing the bristles to retract into the handle in order to protect them when not in use.

Most effective when played on coated heads, as well as being played like sticks, a number of other techniques such as "sweeping" (where the brush is swept across the drumhead) can be used to produce timbres that are not possible with sticks. Players such as Ed Thigpen and Clayton Cameron are renowned for their expertise with the brushes.

Multirods

Multirods are bundles of thin wooden dowels (or rods) that are used like sticks but create a lighter sound with less attack and lower volume. Extremely adaptable in the studio or on quieter gigs, mulitrods are offered by numerous manufacturers in a variety of models. Although most multirod designs are fundamentally the same, there are two main attributes that affect their sound: the number of rods and their diameter (or thickness).

Some manufacturers offer a type of multirod that consists of bundles of plastic rods instead of wooden ones. These are commonly referred to as blasticks and as you would expect, create a different sound than multirods.

Mallets

Traditionally used on other percussion instruments such as tympani or vibraphone, mallets comprise a round head attached to a thin wooden shaft.

Mallet heads are either wrapped or unwrapped depending on their intended application, but most drummers opt for wrapped mallet heads as they are generally softer, making them great for cymbal swells.

Miscellaneous Gear

In addition to the equipment that you've looked at so far, there is a miscellany of other accessories available to you as a drummer.

In this lesson, you will look at some of the other useful gadgets on offer, and learn how they can be used not only to make your life easier, but also help you develop your skills more effectively.

Hearing protection

Drums are very loud and prolonged exposure to them can have a permanent, detrimental effect on your hearing. There is a simple and inexpensive solution to this—hearing protection. The hearing protection most commonly used by drummers are earplugs, which come in a variety of designs and price ranges.

Filter earplugs are tiny devices that offer a "flatter" attenuation. Filter earplugs come in two types—generic and custom. Custom earplugs are molded to the ear of the wearer and therefore have to be specially designed for that individual. The advantage is that they are very comfortable and contain high-quality filters, giving them a very natural sound. The disadvantage is that they are relatively expensive.

Foam earplugs have the advantage of offering a high level of protection at a very low cost. The disadvantage is that it attenuates different frequencies by different amounts, so high frequency, low energy sounds such as cymbals and hi-hats, get blocked out more than the low-frequency, high-energy sounds, such as toms and the bass drum. The result of this is a less natural sound.

Generic filter-earplugs are a good compromise between custom earplugs and foam earplugs. They are designed to fit any ear, offer a more natural sound than foam plugs, but are considerably less expensive than custom plugs.

Drum machines

Many drummers prefer to use drum machines than the more traditional metronomes. The advantage is that they are highly programmable, which allows them to be used in more imaginative ways to enhance practice sessions. For example, you could program percussion loops to play along with, instead of the simple click of the metronome. Of course, they can also be used to create entire drum tracks, so owning one helps develop drum-programing skills too.

Metronomes

A good sense of timing is a prerequisite for any drummer, and a metronome is an invaluable tool for helping to develop this. Virtually all metronomes are electronic, and range from simple designs such as the Korg MA-30 digital metronome, to more sophisticated models such as the Boss DB-88 metronome.

Practice pads

As your neighbors will quickly find out, drums are noisy. Consequently, it is not always possible to practice on a real set, so most drummers own at least one practice pad.

Single pads

Single pads serve as a snare drum, enabling you to work on hand technique relatively quietly. Practice pads come in a variety of designs and materials. Some offer lots of bounce, such as the HQ Realfeel pad. Others, like the MoonGel pad, offer very little bounce. When choosing a pad, there are no rules. Try a few and choose one that feels most comfortable to you.

Sets

Practice pads also come in sets, just like real drumsets, and can be an excellent solution to noise problems. As with single pads, try a few and choose the one that feels most natural.

Electronic Drumsets

Some drummers love them, and some hate them, but no one can disagree that electronic drumsets have come a long way since the introduction of the very first electronic percussion instruments in the 1970s. Offering limitless sonic versatility, today's electronic drumsets consist of three basic components: pads, brain, and hardware.

Hardware

Most electronic kits come mounted on a rack, which makes them compact and portable. Additionally, conventional hardware is needed, such as a bass drum pedal, a stool, and, depending on the model of electronic drumset you choose, a hi-hat stand.

Pads

Pads are the electronic drums and cymbals that you actually play. They convert the force of the strike from a stick, or beater, into an electronic signal that is sent to the drum brain.

Brain

This device receives the analogue electrical signal sent from the pad, and converts it into digital information, triggering the appropriate sound. It lets you assign different sounds to different pads, as well as providing a vast array of editing options.

The Roland TD-12 electronic drumset brain is the central processing unit of the electronic drumset, and can recreate thousands of different sounds.

Trigger
cymbal
pads

Trigger pads

Brain

Snare pad

*The Roland TD-6 is typical
of the electronic drumsets
being manufactured today.*

Kick
trigger
pads

High-hat pedal

Electronic or acoustic?

While electronic drumsets have a long way to go before they can reproduce the complexity of their acoustic counterparts, they do offer some inherent advantages.

•With electronic drums, noise is not a problem, as you control the overall volume of the instrument, even listening back through headphones if you choose.

•They are relatively compact, taking up much less room than an acoustic set.

•Most drum brains have built in metronomes and many allow you to program loops that you can then play along to, making them a great practice tool whatever your skill level.

•They are more portable, which means transporting your drums is less of a problem.

•They offer virtually limitless sonic flexibility, which means, at the turn of a dial, you have literally hundreds of drumsets at your disposal.

Part 2:
Reading and notation

1 Notes and Rests

Written or printed notation is a very common way in which musical information is presented. But the information is only accessible to those who can decode it.

As a student of the drums, your goal should be to assimilate as much musical information as possible. In a world where information is so abundantly available through the Internet or any of the numerous drum books currently available, the ability to read musical notation is an indispensable skill.

The notes

A note is a symbol that represents a sound of a specific length. Take some time to memorize the table below, which shows the most commonly used notes, their different names, and their values (in beats).

Note	American Name	European Name	Value
𝅝	Whole-Note	Semibreve	4 beats
𝅗𝅥	Half-Note	Minim	2 beats
𝅘𝅥	Quarter-Note	Crotchet	1 beat
𝅘𝅥𝅮	Eighth-Note	Quaver	½ beat
𝅘𝅥𝅯	Sixteenth-Note	Semiquaver	¼ beat
𝅘𝅥𝅰	Thirty-second-Note	Demi semiquaver	$1/_8$ beat

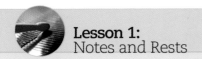

Lesson 1:
Notes and Rests

The rests

A rest is a symbol that represents a silence of a specific length. Take some time to memorize the table below, which shows the most commonly used rests, their names, and their values (in beats).

For the purpose of this book, the notes and rests are in their American names, as this is the most common practice in popular music.

Note	American Name	European Name	Value
—	Whole-Note Rest	Semibreve Rest	4 beats
—	Half-Note Rest	Minim Rest	2 beats
𝄽	Quarter-Note Rest	Crotchet Rest	1 beat
𝄾	Eighth-Note Rest	Quaver Rest	½ beat
𝄿	Sixteenth-Note Rest	Semiquaver Rest	¼ beat
𝅀	Thirty-Second-Note Rest	Demi semiquaver Rest	$\frac{1}{8}$ beat

Beaming

To make music clearer and easier to read, where possible, notes occurring within the same beat have their tails "joined" together. This is called beaming.

For example, this notation...

...becomes much clearer when the notes are beamed like this.

2 Time Signatures, Measures, Barlines, and Clefs

All musical compositions have some type of structure called the form.

The form of a tune is made up of sections. In popular music there are sections such as verses, choruses, and bridges, and it is the specific way in which these are arranged that creates the form of the tune. The sections themselves are made up of smaller units called measures.

Measures

A measure is a collection of strong and weak beats that are counted in a particular way. Measures are separated by barlines. There are three types.

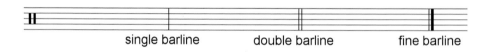

single barline   double barline   fine barline

- Single barlines are the most common and are generally used to separate bars.
- Double barlines are used at the ends of sections.
- Fine (pronounced "fee nay") barlines are used at the end of compositions.

Time signatures

Time signatures can be thought of as fractions. The top number tells you how many counts there are in the measure and the bottom number tells you the value of each count.

So, for example:

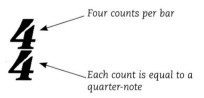

Four counts per bar

Each count is equal to a quarter-note

In popular music 4/4 is by far the most commonly used time signature. In fact, its use is so common that it is often referred to as common time.

Lesson 2:
Time Signatures, Measures, Barlines, and Clefs

Clefs

Notes are symbols that represent sounds of specific lengths, and while the type of note tells you how long the sound lasts, its position on the staff tells you what sound to actually play. The staff is made up of five lines, on which music is written and individually, each line is called a stave. Depending on the instrument, each stave, or space in between the staves represents a different sound or pitch. It is the clef that defines this. The clef is a symbol that appears at the beginning of each line of music and in drumming it is the percussion clef that is used.

There are still some slight variations in the use of the percussion clef, but below is a convention similar to that proposed by the Percussive Arts Society, and the one adopted throughout this book.

bass drum   hi-hat   high tom   mid tom   floor tom   crash cymbal   cross stick   bell of ride cymbal
     snare drum   stepped hi-hat   ride cymbal   open hi-hat

Repeat brackets

Repeat brackets are used when one or more measures of music are to be immediately repeated. The opening bracket occurs at the beginning of the repeated passage and the closing bracket occurs at the end of the repeated passage. Often, if the beginning of the repeated passage is also the beginning of the composition, then the opening bracket is not used.

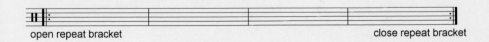

open repeat bracket   close repeat bracket

3 Quarter-Note Reading in 4/4

On the CD
Tracks 82–84

Listen to these exercises being played on the CD.

Now that you are familiar with the different notes and rests, you can begin to apply that knowledge and start reading.

The first exercise is designed to show you how each note relates to another. Notice that each bar contains only one type of note. For example, the first contains one whole-note, the second contains two half-notes, the third four quarter-notes, and so on. In other words, the rate at which you play doubles in each bar all the way up to sixteenth-notes before going down again. Try playing this exercise at a slow tempo, counting aloud throughout. To help, the count is written above each note. When working through the reading exercises in the following lessons, don't forget to refer to the audio examples on the accompanying CD.

Exercise 1 track 82

This symbolizes repeat brackets. This means that when you reach the end of the last bar, you start again at the beginning of the first bar.

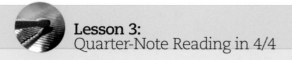

Lesson 3:
Quarter-Note Reading in 4/4

The following exercises involve mixtures of whole-notes, half-notes, quarter-notes, and half-note and quarter-note rests. In examples 2–4 the count is written above each note. In examples 5–7 the count is not written. Take a pencil and try writing the count above each note yourself, then check your version against the audio example on the CD.

Exercise 2

Exercise 3

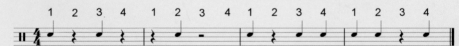

Exercise 4

Exercise 5 track 83

Exercise 6 track 84

4 Eighth-Note Reading in 4/4

On the CD
Track 85

Listen to this exercise being played on the CD.

The exercises in this lesson deal with mixtures of quarter-notes, eighth-notes, and eighth-note rests.

When playing through these exercises, work slowly and count aloud throughout. If possible, it is a very good idea to work with a metronome. This will not only help you play these exercises accurately but also help you develop your internal sense of timing.

Exercise 1

Exercise 2

Exercise 3

Exercise 4 track 85

In this exercise the count is not given. With a pencil, write the count above the staff. Use the previous exercises to help you and then check your version against the audio example on the CD.

On the CD
Track 86

Listen to this exercise being played on the CD.

Dotted Notes 5

So far you have become familiar with the twelve different notes and rests most commonly used in musical notation.

There are occasions when it is necessary to represent sounds (or indeed silences) of different lengths than those represented by these. One of the ways that this is achieved is through the use of dotted notes.

When a note is attended by a dot, the value of that note is increased by 50 percent. So for example, a whole-note has a value of four beats. If it is "dotted" and its value increases by 50 percent, then its new value must be six beats. The table below shows the values of the dotted notes:

Although it is possible to add dots to both sixteenth-notes and thirty-second notes, neither is common, so they have not been included here. As well as the materials introduced previously, the following exercises include dotted quarter notes.

𝅝·	6 beats	𝄻·	6 beats
𝅗𝅥·	3 beats	𝄼·	3 beats
♩·	1½ beats	𝄽·	1½ beats
♪·	¾ beat	𝄾·	¾ beat

Exercise 1 track 86

Exercise 2

Exercise 3

6 Tied Notes

On the CD
Track 87

Listen to this exercise being played on the CD.

In the last lesson you discovered how dots are used to change the value of a note or rest. Another way in which sounds of different durations can be represented is through the use of tied notes.

When two or more notes are tied together, they are treated as a single note whose value is equal to the sum of the individual notes. So for example, if a whole-note (with a value of four beats) is tied to a half-note (with a value of two beats) they would be treated as a single note with a value of six beats (four beats plus two beats).

The table below shows some common combinations of tied notes.

𝅝 ⌣ 𝅗𝅥	6 beats	𝅗𝅥 ⌣ 𝅗𝅥	3 beats	𝅘𝅥 ⌣ 𝅘𝅥	2 beats
𝅘𝅥 ⌣ 𝅘𝅥𝅮	1½ beats	𝅘𝅥𝅮 ⌣ 𝅘𝅥𝅮	1 beat		

The following exercises involve the use of tied quarter-notes and eighth-notes.

Exercise 1 track 87

Exercise 2

Exercise 3

The Sixteenth-Note 7
Alphabet

The exercises in this lesson focus on the ways in which eighth-notes and sixteenth-notes can be combined to create different one-beat figures.

A quarter-note has a value of one beat, which means that it can be represented by any combination of smaller notes, provided that they also add up to exactly one beat.

So for example, two such figures that you are already familiar with, are:

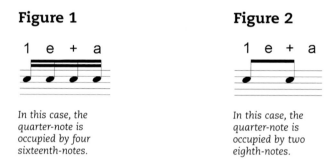

Figure 1

1   e   +   a

In this case, the quarter-note is occupied by four sixteenth-notes.

Figure 2

1   e   +   a

In this case, the quarter-note is occupied by two eighth-notes.

There are a finite number of combinations of notes and rests that add up to one beat. In this lesson you will be introduced to the most common of these.

First though, here are the other one-beat figures that you have already looked at.

Figure 3

1 e + a

Figure 4

1   e   +   a

Figure 5

1   e   +   a

Exercise 1 involves the use of figures 1–5 (see previous page).

Exercise 1 track 88

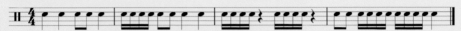

Exercise 2

Figure 6

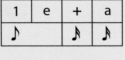

This figure consists of an eighth-note and two sixteenth-notes and involves playing on the beat, the "+," and the "a."

Exercise 1 track 89

Exercise 2

Exercise 3

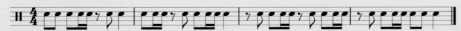

Lesson 7:
The Sixteenth-Note Alphabet

Figure 7

This figures consists of two sixteenth-notes and an eighth-note, and involves playing on the beat, the "e" and the "+."

Exercise 1 track 90

Exercise 2

Exercise 3

Figure 8

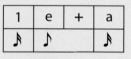

This figure consists of an eighth-note and two sixteenth-notes and involves playing on the beat, the "e," and the "a."

Exercise 1 track 91

Exercise 2

Exercise 3

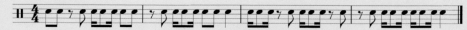

Figure 9

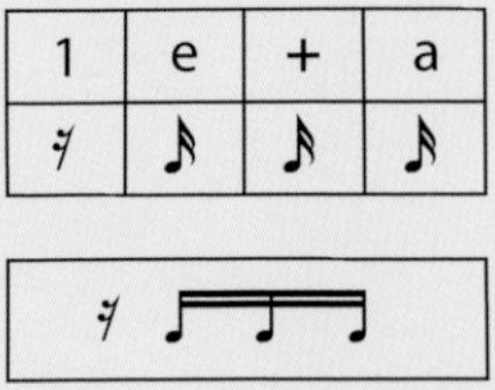

1	e	+	a
𝄾	♪	♪	♪

This figure consists of a sixteenth-note rest, and three sixteenth-notes, and involves playing on the beat, the "e," the "+," and the "a."

Exercise 1 track 92

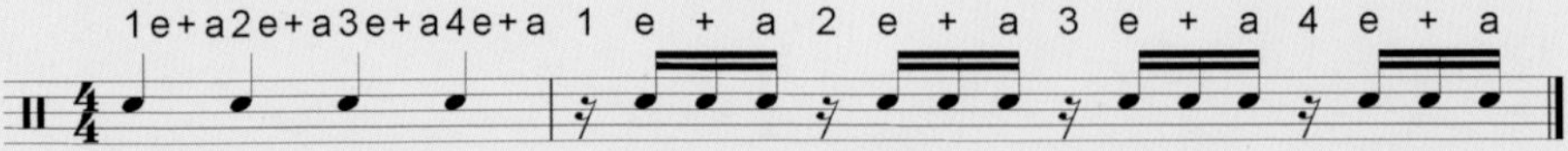

Exercise 2

Exercise 3

Figure 10

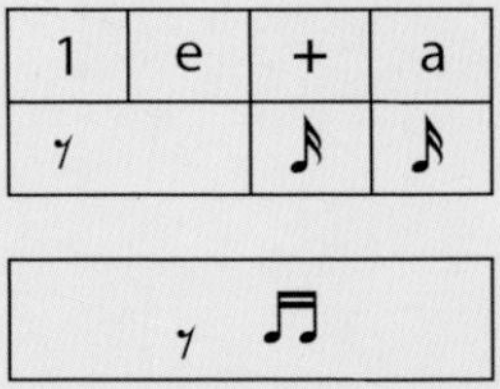

1	e	+	a
𝄾		♪	♪

This figure consists of an eighth-note rest, and two sixteenth-notes, and involves playing on the "+" and the "a."

Exercise 1 track 93

Exercise 2

Exercise 3

Lesson 7:
The Sixteenth-Note Alphabet

Figure 11

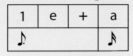

This figure consists of a dotted eighth-note and a sixteenth-note and involves playing on the beat and the "a."

Exercise 1 track 94

Exercise 2

Exercise 3

Figure 12

This figure consists of a sixteenth-note and a dotted eighth-note and involves playing on the beat and the "e."

Exercise 1 track 95

Exercise 2

Exercise 3

Figure 13

This figure consists of a sixteenth-note rest, a sixteenth-note and an eighth-note and involves playing on the "e" and the "+."

Exercise 1 track 96

Exercise 2

Exercise 3

Figure 14

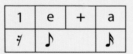

This figure consists of a sixteenth-note rest, an eighth-note, and a sixteenth-note, and involves playing on the "e" and the "a."

Exercise 1 track 97

Exercise 2

Exercise 3

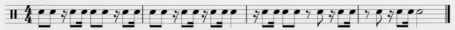

Lesson 7:
The Sixteenth-Note Alphabet

Figure 15

1	e	+	a
𝄾·			♪

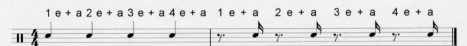

This figure consists of a dotted eighth-note rest and a sixteenth-note, and involves playing on the "a."

Exercise 1 track 98

Exercise 2

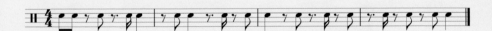

Figure 16

1	e	+	a
𝄾	♪.		

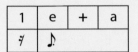

This figure consists of a sixteenth-note rest, and a dotted eighth-note, and involves playing on the "e."

Exercise 1 track 99

Exercise 2

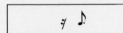

Exercise 3

8 Further Sixteenth-Note Reading in 4/4

The following exercises are all eight bars long and involve mixtures of the one-beat figures introduced in the previous lessons.

Note that no count is written. Start slowly, counting aloud and working one bar at a time. Your aim should be to play all eight bars in succession.

Exercise 1

Exercise 2

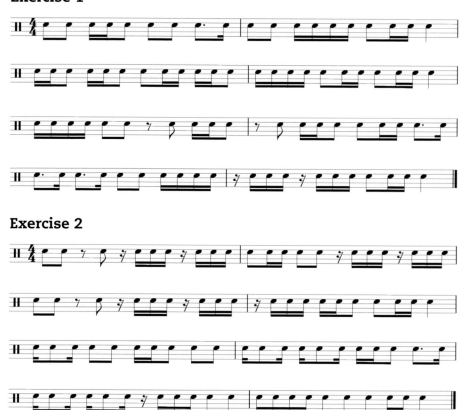

Lesson 8:
Further Sixteenth-Note Reading in 4/4

Exercise 3

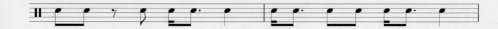

Exercise 4

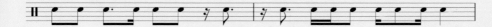

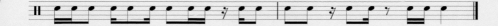

9 Other Time Signatures

So far, all of the reading you have encountered has been in 4/4. Next, you will look at some reading exercises in other time signatures.

Exercises 1–5 are all in 2/4. Remember, time signatures are really just fractions. The top number tells you how many counts there are in a bar, and the bottom number tells you what the value of each count is. So in this case, each bar contains the equivalent of two quarter-notes.

Exercise 1

Exercise 2

Exercise 3

Exercise 4

Exercise 5

Lesson 9:
Other Time Signatures

Exercises 6–10 are all in 3/4. Remember, this means that each bar contains the equivalent of three quarter-notes.

Exercise 6

Exercise 7

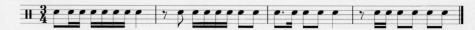

Exercise 8

Exercise 9

Exercise 10

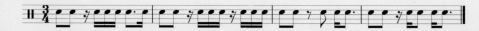

10 Triplets

By now you understand that in 4/4, quarter-notes naturally divide into two eighth-notes, four sixteenth-notes, or even eight thirty-second-notes. These notes can also be combined in different ways to create various one-beat figures.

What happens, however, if you want to divide the beat into something other than two, four, or eight? Say, three, for example. Well in this case, you would have to employ a type of artificial grouping called a triplet.

Artificial grouping refers to the way that rates that do not occur naturally within the time signature are represented. The artificial grouping that enables you to divide the beat into three is called a triplet.

Exercise 1 shows how triplets are written in 4/4. Notice how each beat now seems to contain three eighth-notes.

Exercise 1

It is the number written above the grouping that legitimizes it. It tells you to play three eighth-notes in the time normally reserved for two.

There are numerous counting systems applied to triplets. For the purpose of this book we will use "1 + a 2 + a 3 + a 4 + a," etc. It is important to realise that the "+" and the "a" when counting triplets have nothing to do with the "+" and the "a" when counting sixteenth-notes. The same words are used simply because they are easy to pronounce, especially at faster tempos.

Exercise 2

Lesson 10:
Triplets

Exercise 3

Exercise 4

Exercise 5

Exercise 6

Exercise 7

Exercise 8

11 *Further Triplet Reading*

In the following exercises, two of the most common triplet figures from the previous lesson are combined in different ways.

Work slowly and deliberately at first, counting aloud and ensuring that the notes of the triplet are evenly spaced. As you may have noticed, it is these triplet figures that are the basis for the triplet grooves introduced in Lesson 10.

Exercise 1

Exercise 2

Exercise 3

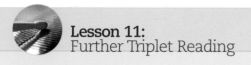

Lesson 11:
Further Triplet Reading

Exercise 4

Exercise 5

Exercise 6

Exercise 7

Exercise 8

Part 3:
The lessons

12 *Grip: Holding the Sticks*

Now it is time to do some playing. The first thing to consider is how to hold the sticks.

Generally speaking, there are two types of grip that are employed on the drumset: traditional grip and matched grip. Traditional grip was originally used by military drummers, who played their snare drums by their sides as they marched.

As a consequence, it became the type of grip used by the earliest drumset players, and is still extremely popular today. Matched grip was originally employed by orchestral percussionists for playing mallet instruments, such as timpani. It later became popular on the drumset.

Traditional grip was used to play drums while marching.

Matched grip was adapted for orchestral drums, such as timpanis.

There are many subtle variations of both traditional and matched grip employed by different players. The guidance opposite describes the most common.

Lesson 12:
Grip: Holding the Sticks

The balance point

The balance point is the point on the body of the stick where, when allowed to pivot freely, the stick will bounce quite naturally. This is called the balance point and is where the fulcrum is created—the part of the grip where the stick pivots.

1: *Hold the stick near the butt and let it rest in the first finger on the right hand. With the left hand, lift the stick a few inches off the drum, and then drop it. The stick will be reluctant to bounce.*

2: *Repeat the process, this time holding the stick about halfway between the tip and the butt. This time the stick will almost want to rest in equilibrium.*

3: *The point between these two extremes is where the stick bounces naturally. This is the balance point and is where the fulcrum is created—it is the part of the grip where the stick pivots.*

Matched grip

In matched grip, both the right hand and left hand hold the stick in the same way.

1: *At the balance point, hold the stick between the pad of the thumb and the first joint on the first finger, creating the fulcrum.*

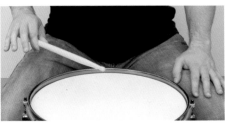 

2: *With the palm facing down, the stick should be in line with the forearm pointing toward the center of the drum.*

3: *Loosely wrap the second, third, and fourth fingers around the stick.*

Traditional grip

In traditional grip, the right hand holds the stick in the same way as for matched grip. However, the left hand holds the stick differently.

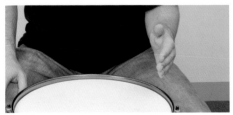 

1: *Here, the palm faces inward, as it would if you were shaking someone's hand.*

2: *The fulcrum is created by holding the stick at the balance point between the thumb and first finger.*

Lesson 12:
Grip: Holding the Sticks

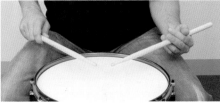

3: *The stick should sit just below the first joint on the third finger.*

4: *Now, wrap the first and second fingers loosely around the stick, with the pad of the thumb touching the first joint on the first finger.*

With any type of grip, it is important not to squeeze the stick. Hold the stick just firmly enough to retain control, but loosely enough to avoid any unnecessary tension in the hands.

Using matched grip

For now, you will use matched grip to work through the exercises in this book. This is because matched grip offers the advantage of only needing to learn one way of holding the stick. Whatever your right hand does, your left hand can simply copy.

Different matched grips

1: *The style of matched grip involving the palm facing down, which means that the thumb is positioned on the side of the stick, is called German position.*

2: *If you rotate your hand 90˚ (degrees) so the palm faces inward and the thumb is on top of the stick, you are holding the stick in the French position.*

3: *In between these two positions, with the thumb at 45˚, you are holding the stick in the American position.*

Each of these positions offers different advantages depending on what you are playing, how you are playing it, and where on the kit you are playing. Therefore, it is important to be equally comfortable in any of these positions. To start with, work through all of the exercises using the German position.

13 Posture: Your Relationship to the Drums

It is important to remember that drumming is a very physical activity, and the way you set up your drumset can have a profound effect on the way you play.

The drums and cymbals should be positioned in line with your body's natural lines of motion, and because each person's body is unique, the way that you set up your drums is a very personal thing.

Stool height

It is important to choose a stool height that is comfortable for you. As a starting point, set the stool a little above knee height so that when you sit down, your thigh is slightly declined.

Snare drum

Next, as if your arms were being pulled up by puppet-strings, raise them in front of you. Your shoulders should still be relaxed so that your elbows are hanging by your side.

Sit upright, looking ahead with your arms hanging loosely by your sides. Your feet should be flat on the floor and you should be comfortable and relaxed. If not, try adjusting the height of the stool slightly until you find the height that is most comfortable for you.

Take the sticks in German grip and hold them at 15° to the horizontal. In this relaxed position, the snare drum should be set up slightly inclined toward you, and so that the tips of the sticks are near the center of the drum and approximately 1.5–2" off the head.

Lesson 13:
Posture: Your Relationship to the Drums

This guidance on positioning your drums will get you started, but be sure to experiment with the positions of each individual drum and cymbal in your set, until you find the ones that suit you most. Remember, the drumset should be set up in away that conforms to your body's natural movement and not the other way around.

Bass drum

If you are right-footed, the bass drum should be placed in front of the snare drum just to the right hand side.

Hi-hat

The hi-hat is set up to the left of the snare drum. It should be at a distance that is comfortable when your left foot is placed on the pedal, and can easily be reached when playing the hi-hat cymbals with the sticks.

The bass drum batter head should be perpendicular to your thigh, and should be just far away enough that when your foot is on the bass drum pedal, your shin is slightly inclined.

The hi-hat should be high enough that when played with the right hand, the left hand has enough space to play the snare drum.

Toms

Starting with the high tom, attach it to the tom arm and position it in front of the snare drum. Set it at an angle that enables the sticks to move in a straight line from the center of the tom to the center of the snare drum, but not so steep that the stick "digs" into the tom head at an angle.

If you have a mid tom, add it next in the same way. Make sure that you can also move unimpeded from the center of the high tom to the center of the mid tom.

Set up the floor tom at roughly the same height as the snare drum, sloping slightly inward, so the sticks can move smoothly from the center of the floor tom to the center of the snare drum, as well as the center of the mid tom.

Lesson 13:
Posture: Your Relationship to the Drums

Cymbals

Both the ride and the crash should be high enough that when they are struck they move freely, and do not hit anything on the drumset, such as the rims of the toms.

Place the crash cymbal on the cymbal stand and position it in between the hi-hat and the high tom tilted slightly inward. Adjust the height so it is in a position that feels natural when played with the sticks.

Place the ride cymbal on a cymbal stand and position it to the right of the mid tom, tilted in so that your right hand can comfortably play the tip of the stick on the bow of the cymbal. You may have to play the ride cymbal for several minutes at a time, so it must be in a position that it can be played without any tension building up in the shoulders or arms.

14 Dynamics

Dynamics is the aspect of music that relates to volume or loudness of a note and, for drummers, it is an indispensable way of shaping musical phrases. There are many different types of dynamic devices that are commonly used.

Dynamic levels
There are six dynamic levels, ranging from very soft to very loud. On paper, these are represented by dynamic markings, which are written in lower case italics.

Crescendo
This is a gradual increase in loudness occurring between any two dynamic levels.

Decrescendo (or Diminuendo)
This a gradual decrease in loudness occurring between any two dynamic levels.

Accents and ghost notes
This is the most common use of dynamics on the drumset and involves the use of loud notes (accents) and quiet notes (ghost notes) to shape musical phrases.

Stick height
Because of the relationship between the distance a stick travels and the force with which it strikes the drum, one of the most effective ways of playing accurately at different dynamic levels, is to equate each level to a specific stick height.

In practice, you simply divide the 90° range of motion between the stick in its vertical position and the stick in its horizontal position (when it is in contact with the drum) into six 15° increments, each one relating to one of the six dynamic levels.

Dynamic marking	Name	Dynamic level	Stick height
ff	fortissimo	very loud	90°
f	forte	loud	75°
mf	mezzo-forte	moderately loud	60°
mp	mezzo-piano	moderately soft	45°
p	piano	soft	30°
pp	pianissimo	very soft	15°

Lesson 14:
Dynamics

Stick at 15° (pp)

Stick at 30° (p)

Stick at 45° (mp)

Stick at 60° (mf)

Stick at 75° (f)

Stick at 90° (ff)

For the purposes of the exercises in this book, you will be focusing predominantly on the use of accents and ghost notes, which use two dynamic levels: fortissimo and pianissimo.

15 *The Strokes*

To execute phrases involving fortissimo and pianissimo (see previous page), you will employ a number of different strokes.

You need to master these strokes with both hands before moving on. In order to do so, work slowly and practice each one daily, working on one hand at time. You are striving for consistency and accuracy in the start and end positions of each stroke, and to ensure a smooth, linear, relaxed motion in between, which will result in the desired sound. When working on these types of materials, a knowledgeable drum tutor will be able to offer additional guidance and supervision.

The tap stroke (T)

This stroke starts in the low position (15°), and ends in the low position (15°). The tap stroke creates a ghost note (pp) and because it ends in the low position, it prepares you to play another ghost note.

The full stroke (F)

This stroke starts in the high position (90°) and ends in the high position (90°). The full stroke creates an accent (ff) and prepares you to play another accent.

Lesson 15:
The Strokes

The up stroke (U)

This stroke starts in the low position (15°) and ends in the high position (90°). The up stroke creates a ghost note (pp).

The down stroke (D)

This stroke starts in the high position (90°) and ends in the low position (15°). The down stroke results in an accent (ff), but prepares you to play a ghost note.

16 *Putting it Together: One-Handed Sequences*

On the CD
Tracks 1–6

Want to read music? See
Reading and Notation
page 38.

Now that you have mastered the basic strokes, it is time to start putting them together to create some musical phrases. To begin with, you will look at different sequences of these motions involving one hand at a time.

Starting with the right hand only, practice all of these patterns very slowly, at first concentrating on smooth motions, accurate and consistent stick heights, and an even rhythm. When you have mastered each of these with the right hand, go back and review them with the left hand. It is very important that you can comfortably execute all of these exercises with either hand before proceeding onward.

Exercise 1 track 1

This sequence involves the down stroke (D), and the up stroke (U), and the accent is played every two notes

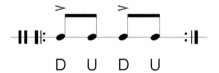

D   U   D   U

Exercise 2 track 2

As well as the up and down strokes, this sequence involves the tap stroke (T), and the accent is played every three notes.

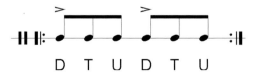

D   T   U   D   T   U

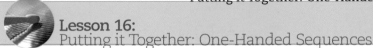

Lesson 16:
Putting it Together: One-Handed Sequences

Exercise 3 track 3

This sequence involves up, down, and tap strokes, and the accent is played every four notes.

D T T U D T T U

Exercise 4 track 4

As well as the up and down strokes, this sequence involves the full stroke (F), which creates a three-note pattern with two accents.

F D U F D U

Exercise 5 track 5

This involves all four strokes and creates a four-note pattern with two accents.

F D T U F D T U

Exercise 6 track 6

This sequence involves full, down, and up strokes, and creates a four-note pattern with three accents.

F F D U F F D U

17 Putting it Together: Two-Handed Sequences

On the CD
Tracks 7–12

Want to read music?
See Reading and
Notation page 38.

*Having mastered the one-handed sequences
from the previous lesson, it is now time to look
at patterns involving two hands. As with the
previous exercises, work very slowly at first,
maintaining an even rhythm, smooth motions,
and accurate and consistent stick heights.*

All of these patterns involve the use of both hands, so in addition to the
sequence of strokes, you must now also be concerned with the sequence of
right- and left-hand notes. In drumming, this is called "the sticking."

Most often, stickings are written underneath the staff and are described by
the use of letters. "R" represents a note played with the right hand, and "L"
represents a note played with the left hand. In the following exercises the
same sticking is used throughout—right, left, right, left, etc. This is probably
the most common of all stickings and is referred to as "single strokes."

Exercise 1 track 7

This is a four-note sequence using down strokes and up strokes in the right hand,
and tap strokes in the left hand.

```
r  l  r  l  r  l  r  l
D  T  U  T  D  T  U  T
```

Exercise 2 track 8

Again, down strokes and up strokes are used in the right hand, and tap strokes
are used in the left hand, this time creating a six-note pattern.

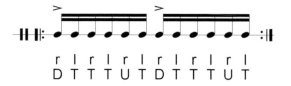

```
r  l  r  l  r  l  r  l  r  l  r  l
D  T  T  T  U  T  D  T  T  T  U  T
```

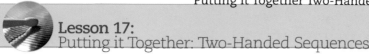

Lesson 17:
Putting it Together: Two-Handed Sequences

Exercise 3 track 9
In this six-note pattern the full strokes are used in the right hand.

```
r  l  r  l  r  l  r  l  r  l
F  T  D  T  U  T  F  T  D  T  U  T
```

Exercise 4 track 10
Again, full strokes, down strokes, and up strokes are used in the right hand, while tap strokes are used in the left hand, creating an eight-note pattern.

```
r  l  r  l  r  l  r  l  r  l  r  l  r  l
F  T  D  T  T  U  T  F  T  D  T  T  U  T
```

Exercise 5 track 11
In the previous exercises the left hand has only played tap strokes. Here, down and up strokes are introduced into the left hand part, creating a six-note pattern with a double accent.

```
r  l  r  l  r  l  r  l  r  l  r  l
D  D  T  T  U  U  D  D  T  T  U  U
```

Exercise 6 track 12
Again, down strokes, tap strokes, and up strokes are used in both hands, creating an eight-note pattern with a double accent.

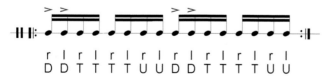

```
r  l  r  l  r  l  r  l  r  l  r  l  r  l
D  D  T  T  T  U  U  D  D  T  T  T  U  U
```

Once you are comfortable with these exercises it is very important to review them with the sticking inverted. This means that all right-hand notes become left-hand notes and all left-hand notes become right-hand notes.

18 Accented Sixteenth-Notes

On the CD
Tracks 13–16

Want to read music?
See Reading and
Notation page 38.

You will now develop the ideas introduced with the two-handed sequences and apply the motions to musical phrases on the drumset.

The following exercises are in 4/4, and involve different permutations of accents, using single-strokes at a sixteenth-note rate.

Exercise 1 track 13

```
R L R L R L R L R L R L R L R L
D T U T D T U T D T U T D T U T
```

Exercise 2 track 14

```
R L R L R L R L R L R L R L R L
T D T U T D T U T D T U T D T U
```

Exercise 3 track 15

```
R L R L R L R L R L R L R L R L
U T D T U T D T U T D T U T D T
```

Exercise 4 track 16

```
R L R L R L R L R L R L R L R L
T U T D T U T D T U T D T U T D
```

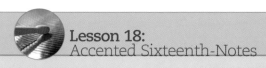

Lesson 18:
Accented Sixteenth-Notes

Exercise 5

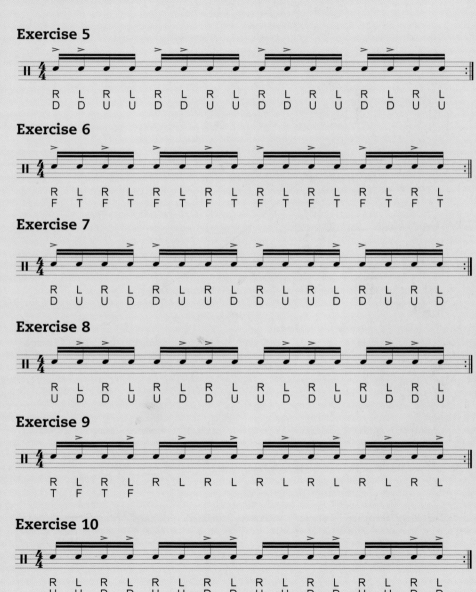

```
R  L  R  L  R  L  R  L  R  L  R  L  R  L  R  L
D  D  U  U  D  D  U  U  D  D  U  U  D  D  U  U
```

Exercise 6

```
R  L  R  L  R  L  R  L  R  L  R  L  R  L  R  L
F  T  F  T  F  T  F  T  F  T  F  T  F  T  F  T
```

Exercise 7

```
R  L  R  L  R  L  R  L  R  L  R  L  R  L  R  L
D  U  U  D  D  U  U  D  D  U  U  D  D  U  U  D
```

Exercise 8

```
R  L  R  L  R  L  R  L  R  L  R  L  R  L  R  L
U  D  D  U  U  D  D  U  U  D  D  U  U  D  D  U
```

Exercise 9

```
R  L  R  L  R  L  R  L  R  L  R  L  R  L  R  L
T  F  T  F
```

Exercise 10

```
R  L  R  L  R  L  R  L  R  L  R  L  R  L  R  L
U  U  D  D  U  U  D  D  U  U  D  D  U  U  D  D
```

19 Accented Sixteenth Studies

On the CD
Track 17

Want to read music?
See Reading and
Notation page 38.

The following exercises are short etudes that mix up the different accent patterns introduced in the previous lesson.

As in the last lesson, the sticking used is single-strokes but in this case the sequence of motions is not given. Therefore, work slowly and concentrate on each bar individually at first. Then, try playing each line separately before attempting to play the whole piece.

Exercise 1 track 17

R L R L R L R L R L R L R L R L R L R L R L R L R L R L R L R L

R L R L R L R L R L R L R L R L R L R L R L R L R L R L R L R L

R L R L R L R L R L R L R L R L R L R L R L R L R L R L R L R L

R L R L R L R L R L R L R L R L R L R L R L R L R L R L R L R L

Lesson 19:
Accented Sixteenth Studies

Exercise 2

R L R L R L R L R L R L R L R L R L R L R L R L R L R L R L R L

R L R L R L R L R L R L R L R L R L R L R L R L R L R L R L R L

R L R L R L R L R L R L R L R L R L R L R L R L R L R L R L R L

R L R L R L R L R L R L R L R L R L R L R L R L R L R L R L R L

20 Accented Triplets

On the CD
Tracks 18–20

Want to read music?
See Reading and
Notation page 38.

*Now that you are comfortable applying accents to
sixteenth-note phrases, it is time to apply them to
another common rate—triplets.*

If you are unfamiliar with the concept of triplets, an
explanation can be found in Lesson 10. Once again, the
sticking used is single-strokes, and in this case the sequence
of motions is provided. In these exercises, the accents often
switch between the right and left hands, so work slowly at
first, maintaining an even rhythm, smooth motions, and
consistent stick heights.

Exercise 1 track 18

| R | L | R | L | R | L | R | L | R | L | R | L |
| D | U | T | D | U | T | D | U | T | D | U | T |

Exercise 2 track 19

| R | L | R | L | R | L | R | L | R | L | R | L |
| T | D | U | T | D | U | T | D | U | T | D | U |

Exercise 3 track 20

| R | L | R | L | R | L | R | L | R | L | R | L |
| U | T | D | U | T | D | U | T | D | U | T | D |

Lesson 20:
Accented Triplets

Exercise 4

| R | L | R | L | R | L | R | L | R | L |
| D | F | U | D | F | U | D | F | U | D | F | U |

Exercise 5

| R | L | R | L | R | L | R | L | R | L |
| F | U | D | F | U | D | F | U | D | F | U | D |

Exercise 6

| R | L | R | L | R | L | R | L | R | L |
| U | D | F | U | D | F | U | D | F | U | D | F |

21 Accented Triplet Studies

On the CD
Track 21

Want to read music?
See Reading and
Notation page 38..

As with the sixteenth-note exercises, the next step is to mix the different accent lines introduced in the previous lesson.

The following exercises are short etudes that deal with mixing different accent lines. As before, the sticking used is single-strokes, but in this case the sequence of motions is not given. Therefore, work slowly and concentrate on each bar individually at first. Then try playing each line separately before attempting to play the whole piece.

Exercise 1 track 21

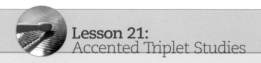

Lesson 21:
Accented Triplet Studies

Exercise 2

R L R L R L R L R L R L R L R L R L R L R L R L R L R L R L R L

R L R L R L R L R L R L R L R L R L R L R L R L R L R L R L R L

R L R L R L R L R L R L R L R L R L R L R L R L R L R L R L R L

R L R L R L R L R L R L R L R L R L R L R L R L R L R L R L R L

22 The Rudiments

Until the end of the nineteenth century, drumming was used as an effective method of directing troops in battlefield combat. In an era when weaponry was inefficient, immobile, and often unreliable, it could require up to thirteen commands to load and fire a canon.

Historically, troops were directed in battle using a series of short codes, played on the snare drum. As well as being accurately executed, the meaning of these codes had to be unambiguous and consequently a "drumming language" evolved. The "words" in this language are known today as The Rudiments. With the advent of modern warfare, the snare drum became impractical and redundant in this role. However, the art of rudimental drumming endured. As well as becoming the basis of vocabulary on the drumset, it can be heard today through the various pipe bands and drum corps that exist around the world.

Military snare drummer using traditional grip.

The drummers of the Scottish pipe bands are masters of rudimental playing.

the development of hand technique. Thirdly, they are a source of creative and conceptual influence that can be extremely useful in developing individual and original ideas on the drums.

Traditionally, there were twenty-six rudiments that were most commonly practiced. These were established in 1933 by the National Association of Rudimental Drummers (NARD) in the USA and consequently became known as the "Twenty-six American Rudiments." Later, the Percussive Arts Society (PAS) took responsibility for the organization of the rudiments and established the "Forty International Rudiments," incorporating rudiments from the Swiss drumming tradition as well as some newer patterns.

As an introduction to the rudiments, in the following lessons you will look at some of the more basic rudimental patterns. However, a complete list of all Forty International Rudiments can be downloaded free of charge from the Percussive Arts Society website listed at the back of this book.

For drumset players the rudiments are of particular significance. Firstly, they are deeply and inextricably connected to the history and evolution of the language of modern drumset playing. Secondly, they are highly effective catalysts for

23 The Single-Stroke Roll

On the CD
Track 22

Want to read music?
See Reading and
Notation page 38.

*Although challenging to execute effectively, this
rudiment is one of the most fundamental patterns
played on the drums, so the ability to play a
fast, controlled single-stroke roll is indispensable.
The single-stroke roll is number 1 in the PAS
International Rudiments.*

Single-stroke roll

R L R L R L R L R L R L R L R L

So far, all of the motions that you have studied have involved the use of the wrist
as the primary way of articulating the stick. This works well where power and
control are needed, but it is only really effective up to certain speeds. In order to
develop a good, fast single-stroke roll, you will now look at another common way
of articulating the stick—through the use of the fingers. The idea is to get the stick
bouncing (rather like a basket ball) by "flicking" the stick with your fingers. Notice
that there is minimal movement in the wrist, but that the stick moves almost
entirely by pivoting at the fulcrum. This can be tricky at first so be patient and
stay relaxed—it is very important not to tense-up or grip too tightly.

1: *start with the
stick at 45°, with
fingers slightly
open.*

2: *Using the
fingers, give
the stick a flick,
causing it to
pivot in the
fulcrum, striking
the drum.*

3: *Remain
relaxed, letting
the stick bounce
back to the start
position.*

4: *Without
letting the stick
stop, repeat the
action.*

5: *The idea is to
get the stick to
"bounce."*

Lesson 23:
The Single-Stroke Roll

Once you are comfortable bouncing the stick with the fingers in either hand, try the following exercise designed to help you put the hands together and begin creating the single-stroke roll.

Exercise 1 track 22

R R R R L R L R L R L   R R R R L R L R L R L

R R R R L R L R L R L   R L R L R L R L R L R L R L

Exercise 2

L L L L L R L R L R L R   L L L L L R L R L R L R

L L L L L R L R L R L R   L R L R L R L R L R L R L R

24 The Double-Stroke Roll

On the CD
Track 23

Want to read music?
See Reading and
Notation page 38.

The double-stroke roll is another very common and indispensable pattern on the drums. In this rudiment, the roll is generated by playing two notes in each hand. The double-stroke roll is number 6 in the PAS International Rudiments.

Double-stroke roll

R L R L R L R L R L R L R L

One of the most effective ways of executing fast, controlled double-strokes is through a combination of wrist and finger motion.

These motions are challenging so be very patient. Remember, it is the quality of the motion, and not the speed with which it is acquired that will lead to the necessary control and technical facility. Focus on staying very relaxed throughout.

1: *Start with the stick horizontally a couple of inches off the drum.*

2: *Retaining control at the fulcrum, open the grip allowing the stick to strike the head. This gives you the first note of the double.*

3: *The trick here is to allow the stick to bounce back, pivoting at the fulcrum.*

4: *When it does, pull the fingers in causing the stick to "snap" back into the head.*

5: *This gives you the second-note of the double.*

Lesson 24:
The Double-Stroke Roll

Once you feel comfortable with this motion, take a look at the following exercises. Notice how the second note of each double-stroke is accented. Practicing this carefully will ensure that your double-stroke roll remains even as you develop the ability to play faster.

Exercise 1 track 23

Exercise 2

25 The Roll Rudiments

On the CD
Track 24

Want to read music?
See Reading and
Notation page 38.

The following rudiments are developed from the double-stroke roll, and—once mastered—can be highly effective when applied to the drumset.

They involve the use of double-strokes to create a subdivision in the phrase, and derive their names from the number of notes in the pattern. The stickings for each pattern are provided, and in the case of the seven-stroke roll, which does not naturally alternate, be sure to practice the pattern leading with both the right and left hands, as indicated.

The five-stroke roll track 24

R R L L R   L L R R L

The six-stroke roll

R L L R R L   R L L R R L

The seven-stroke roll

R R L L R R L   R R L L R R L
L L R R L L R   L L R R L L R

On the CD
Track 25

Want to read music?
See Reading and
Notation page 38

Flam Rudiments 26

A flam is a rudiment consisting of a single, loud primary stroke in the leading hand, preceded by a quieter grace note in the other hand. The space between the two notes has no specific rhythmic value, but should be extremely close together, almost creating a single "broader" note. Because of this, the grace note is said to ornament the primary note.

A very effective way to execute flams is to play an up stroke and a down stroke simultaneously. If both motions are started at the same time, the hand playing the up stroke has less distance to travel, so will strike the drum slightly before the hand playing the down stroke. In this case, the primary note is being played by the louder down stroke and the grace note is being played by the quieter up stroke. The flam is number 20 in the PAS International Rudiments.

Flam track 25

Flam tap

This rudiment is a two-note pattern that involves a right-handed flam followed by a right-handed tap. It then immediately alternates with a left-handed flam followed by a left-handed tap, as shown below.

Flam accent

This rudiment is a three-note pattern that involves a right-handed flam, a left-handed tap, and a right-handed tap. It then immediately alternates with a left-handed flam, a right-handed tap, and a left-handed tap.

27 **Drag Rudiments**

On the CD
Track 26

Want to read music?
See Reading and
Notation page 38.

A drag is a rudiment consisting of a single, loud primary stroke in the leading hand, preceded by two quieter grace notes in the other hand.

The space between the three notes has no specific rhythmic value, but should be close together. Because of this, the grace notes are said to ornament the primary note.

Drag track 26

LL R   RR L

Single drag-tap

LL R   L RR L   R

Single ratamacue

LL R L R L RR L R L R

Double ratamacue

LL R LL R L R L RR L   L R L R

Triple ratamacue

LL R LL R LL R L R L RR L RR L RR L R L R

On the CD
Tracks 27–29
Want to read music?
See Reading and
Notation page 38.

The Diddle Rudiments 28

The diddle rudiments all involve the use of both single and double strokes, and each one is characterized by a specific sticking.

Unlike the roll rudiments, the doubles are not used to create a subdivision in the phrases, but are actually played at the same rate as the singles. The most well known of all the diddle rudiments is the single paradiddle.

The single paradiddle

This rudiment is usually written as sixteenth-notes and involves an accent every four notes, which is created by the use of a specific sticking: "RLRR LRLL."

Exercise 1 track 27

R	L	R	R	L	R	L	L	R	L	R	R	L	R	L	L
D	U	T	T	D	U	T	T	D	U	T	T	D	U	T	T

The following exercises show all of the permutations of the single paradiddle starting with a right-hand note. Because of this, the accent moves relative to the beat. These patterns can be very useful when applied to the drumset, and so should be carefully practiced.

Exercise 2

R	L	R	L	L	R	L	R	R	L	R	L	L	R	L	R
T	D	U	T	T	D	U	T	T	D	U	T	T	D	U	T

Exercise 3

R	R	L	R	L	L	R	L	R	R	L	R	L	L	R	L
T	T	D	U	T	T	D	U	T	T	D	U	T	T	D	U

Exercise 4

```
R  L  L  R  L  R  R  L  R  L  L  R  L  R  R  L
U  T  T  D  U  T  T  D  U  T  T  D  U  T  T  D
```

Double paradiddle

Another common diddle rudiment, the double paradiddle is a six-note pattern that consists of four singles and a double.

Exercise 5 track 28

```
R  L  R  L  R  R  L  R  L  R  L  L
F  T  D  U  T  T  F  T  D  U  T  T
```

The paradiddle-diddle

The paradiddle-diddle is a six-note pattern involving two singles and two doubles. The pattern does not naturally alternate, so be sure to practice the pattern leading with the left hand.

Exercise 6 track 29

```
R  L  R  R  L  L  R  L  R  R  L  L
D  T  T  U  T  T  D  T  T  U  T  T
```

Lesson 28:
The Diddle Rudiments

The following exercises deal with mixtures of both the double paradiddle and the paradiddle-diddle.

Exercise 7

```
R L R L R R L R L R L L    R L R L R R L R L R L L
F T D U T T F T D U T T    F T D U T T F T D U T T
```

```
R L R R L L R L R R L L    R L R R L L R L R R L L
D T T U T T D T T U T T    D T T U T T D T T U T T
```

Exercise 8

```
R L R L R R L R L L R R    L R L R L L R L R R L L
F T D U T T D T T U T T    F T D U T T D T T U T T
```

The following exercises deal with mixtures of all of the diddle rudiments introduced so far. These types of materials are very useful when applied to the drumset and provide the basis for a lot of the musical vocabulary on the instrument. They can be very challenging at first so work slowly and patiently, and concentrate on maintaining an even rhythm, smooth motions and consistent stick heights.

Exercise 9

```
R L R R L R L L R R L R L L R R    L R L L R L R R L L R L R R L L
```

Lesson 28:
The Diddle Rudiments

Exercise 10

R L R R L L R L R R L R L L R R L R L L R R L R L L R L R R L L

Exercise 11

R L R R L L R L R R L L R L R R L R L L R R L R L L R R L R L L

Exercise 12

R L R R L R L R L L R L R L R R L R L L R L R L R R L R L R L L

Exercise 13

R L R L R R L R L L R L R L R R L R L R L L R L R R L R L R L L

Exercise 14

R L R R L L R L R R L L R L R R L R L L R R L R L L R R L R L L

Foot Techniques 28

There are numerous techniques employed by different drummers to articulate the bass drum pedal. Some drummers opt to leave the beater on the drumhead, and others prefer to let it bounce back.

The techniques described in this lesson are not the only ones used to play on the bass drum, but once mastered, they are highly effective and will facilitate the level of control necessary to work through the exercises in this book.

Flat-footed technique

This is the most basic way of articulating the bass drum pedal and has the advantage of being easy to learn, and—when mastered—offers a high degree of control at low volumes. With this technique the heel stays on the plate, and the pedal is articulated by the ankle.

1: *Start with the foot completely relaxed resting on the footplate with the toes close to the end. Notice that even when relaxed, the weight of the foot will cause the beater to move a little closer to the head.*

2: *Keeping the foot in contact with the footplate, raise it slightly, allowing the beater to move away from the head.*

3: *In one quick smooth movement, press the foot down on the footplate causing the beater to change direction and strike the head.*

4: *As soon as the beater strikes the head, relax the foot so that the beater returns to the start position.*

This technique should be executed as one smooth motion. This is important because the necessary power is generated by "whipping" the beater into the head.

Heel-up technique

This is a more challenging technique that involves the use of the complete leg, causing the heel to leave the plate. The advantage of this technique is that it offers enhanced power, speed, and volume. The technique really comprises two motions: the leg stroke and the foot/leg stroke.

Leg stroke

This motion enables you to play a powerful, quick, and controlled stroke and is used to play single bass drum notes.

When mastered, this technique should be executed as one smooth "hopping" motion. As with the flat-footed technique, the necessary power is generated by "whipping" the beater into the head.

1: Start with foot completely relaxed about two-thirds of the way up the footplate. Again, notice that even when relaxed, the weight of the foot will cause the beater to move a little closer to the head.

2: Using the thigh, raise the leg, keeping the ankle loose so that the ball of the foot stays in contact with the footplate. Notice that the beater will move away from the head.

3: With the foot relaxed, drop the leg causing the ball of the foot to press down on the footplate and the beater to strike the head.

4: Because the foot is relaxed, the beater will move back off the head and the weight of the foot on the footplate will bring the beater to rest.

Lesson 29:
Foot Techniques

Foot/leg stroke

To play quick doubles on the bass drum we combine the leg stroke with another motion called the foot stroke.

1: *Start with foot completely relaxed about two-thirds of the way up the footplate. Again, notice that even when relaxed, the weight of the foot will cause the beater to move a little closer to the head.*

2: *Using the thigh, raise the leg, keeping the ankle loose so that the ball of the foot stays in contact with the footplate. Notice that the beater will move away from the head.*

3: *At the top of the leg-stroke, use the ball of the foot to push on the footplate causing the beater to strike the bass drum, so giving you the first note.*

4: *This motion is articulated by the ankle so there should be no movement of the knee at this point and the foot should be relaxed, allowing the beater to bounce back off the head.*

5: *Drop the leg, causing the ball of the foot to press down on the footplate and the beater to strike the head.*

6: *Because the foot is relaxed, the beater will move back off the head, and the weight of the foot on the footplate will bring the beater to rest.*

The hi-hat

The techniques employed by the left foot to play the hi-hat are slightly different than those used on the bass drum. For the exercises in Lesson 32 involving open hi-hat notes, use the flat-footed technique. This gives more control over the distance between the hi-hat cymbals, enabling you to control the sound.

For the exercises involving 4-way coordination, use a version of the heel-up technique. This will enable you to play faster, and with more power, generating greater volume from the hi-hat cymbals.

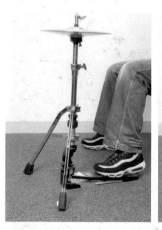

Lesson 29:
Foot Techniques

Double bass drums

All of the exercises in this book are designed for a standard five-piece set with one bass drum.

However, since the 1950s drummers such as Louis Bellson and Sam Woodyard have been exploring the use of two bass drums.

More synonymous nowadays with heavy rock and metal than jazz, drummers across all genres are incorporating double bass drum techniques into their playing. The introduction of a practical double bass drum pedal by Drum Workshop in the 1980s means it is possible to employ double bass drum techniques on a single bass drum.

Similarly, innovation in the design of hi-hats has seen the introduction of the cable hi-hat, which enables the pedal to be placed much further away from the cymbals.

Multi-pedal set-ups

The innovations in the design and manufacture of foot pedals described left have led to some interesting and impressive artistic innovations on the drumset too. Pioneered by drummers such as Terry Bozzio and Thomas Lang, multiple pedal set-ups are now much more common, enabling players to execute complex multi-timbre patterns in the feet.

Thomas Lang and his multiple pedal set-up.

30 Eighth-Note Grooves with Eighth-Note Bass Drum Patterns

On the CD
Track 30–31

Want to read music?
See Reading and
Notation page 38.

Coordination is an essential skill for any drummer, enabling him or her to create grooves by playing different parts of the drum set simultaneously. In this lesson, you are going to begin developing this skill by looking at eighth-note grooves.

The parts of the drum set you will be using are the:

Hi-hat
Played with the right hand
Snare drum
Played with the left hand
Bass drum
Played with the right foot

Playing these patterns involves the use of three limbs. For this reason, this type of coordination is called "3-way coordination."

Exercise 1 track 30

1: Sitting at the drums with the sticks in your hands, start by slowly counting out "1 + 2 + 3 + 4 +," and repeat over and over again, making sure all the counts are even. When you are comfortable with this, play a single hi-hat note on every count with the right hand. The hi-hat part that you are now playing is the basis of all the grooves that you will learn in this section.

Written out, it looks like this.

Lesson 30:
Eighth-Note Grooves with Eighth-Note Bass Drum Patterns

2: While still playing the hi-hat part, play a bass drum note on every count of "1," and every count of "3." This means that the hi-hat and bass drum will be played together on beats "1" and "3."

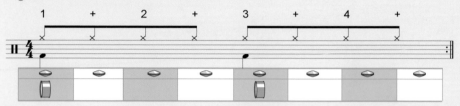

3: Next, while still playing the hi-hat and bass drum, play a snare drum note with the left hand on every count of "2" and "4."

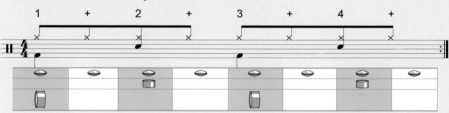

Congratulations—you are now playing drums. Now continue by applying this process to another groove with a different bass drum pattern.

Exercise 2 track 31
1. Start with the hi-hat.

2: Add the bass drum. Play the bass drum on beats "1," and "3," but in this groove there is an additional bass drum on the "+" of "3."

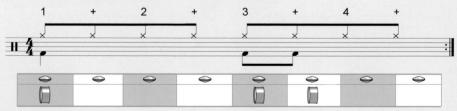

3: Finally, play the snare drum on "2" and "4" to complete the groove.

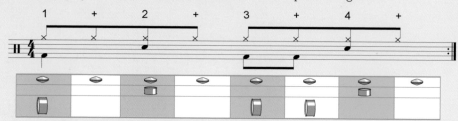

Apply this process to the following grooves.

Exercise 3

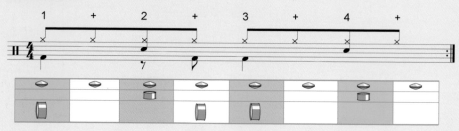

Exercise 4

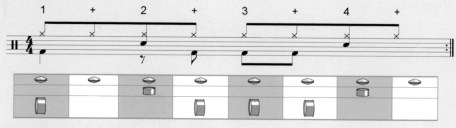

Exercise 5

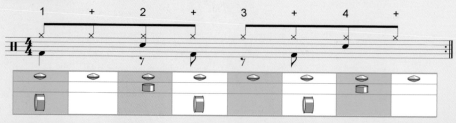

Lesson 30:
Eighth-Note Grooves with Eighth-Note Bass Drum Patterns

Exercise 6

Exercise 7

Exercise 8

Exercise 9

What's in a groove?

See if you can notice these things the next time you are listening to music.
- In these grooves, the basic time is created by the snare drum and bass drum.
- Playing the snare drum on beats "2" and "4" like this is called the "backbeat."
- It is the role of the bass drum to lock in with the bass guitar part.
- The high-frequency sound of the hi-hat ties the snare drum and bass drum parts together.

31 Eighth-Note Grooves with Eighth-Note Snare Drum Variations

On the CD
Tracks 32–33

Want to read music?
See Reading and
Notation page 38.

In the previous lesson, you began developing your 3-way coordination by playing different bass drum figures against a constant hi-hat and snare drum pattern. In this lesson you will continue developing your coordination, this time by playing different figures in the snare drum.

The following exercises feature the same bass drum patterns as those in the previous lesson but an extra snare drum is added on the "+" of "4." Consequently, the hi-hat and snare drum part looks like this:

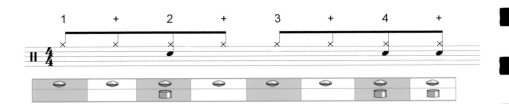

Start working very slowly and don't forget to count aloud. Make sure that you're comfortable playing the hi-hat and snare drum part before moving on.

Exercise 1 track 32

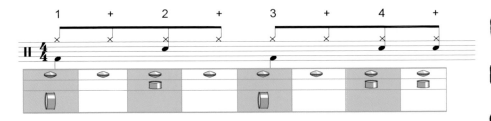

Lesson 31:
Eighth-Note Grooves with Eighth-Note Snare Drum Variations

Exercise 2 track 33

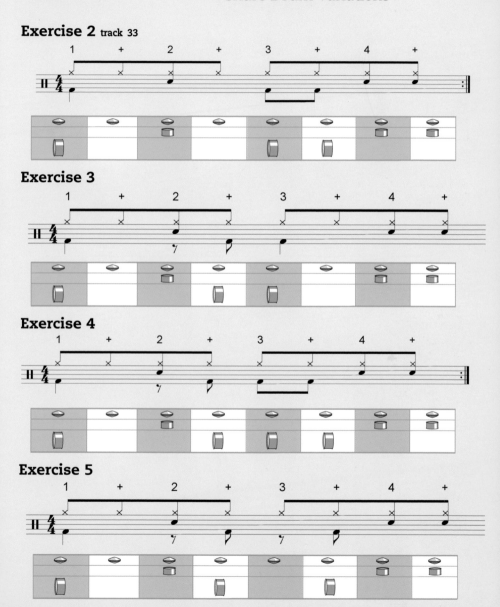

Exercise 3

Exercise 4

Exercise 5

In the following exercises, you are no longer playing an extra snare drum note on the "+" of "4" but instead on the "+" of "1." Notice how this affects the feel of these grooves.

In these exercises, only the musical notation and the count are provided.

Exercise 6

Exercise 7

Exercise 8

Exercise 9

Exercise 10

Lesson 31:
Eighth-Note Grooves with Eighth-Note
Snare Drum Variations

In the following exercises, both of the previous ideas are combined so you are playing extra snare drum notes on the "+" of "1" and the "+" of "4." Only the musical notation is provided here.

Exercise 11

Exercise 12

Exercise 13

Exercise 14

Exercise 15

32 Eighth-Note Grooves with Open Hi-hat

On the CD
Track 34

Want to read music?
See Reading and
Notation page 38.

One of the most common ways to embellish these types of grooves is through the use of open hi-hat notes. This involves opening the hi-hat cymbals slightly with the left foot just before playing them with the stick. The result is a long sustained sound.

When opening the hi-hats, keep the foot flat on the pedal, pivoting at the ankle without raising the knee. This will give you more control over the distance between the cymbals, and consequently, more control over the sound. Normally the hi-hats would be closed again in unison with the next right-hand note.

In the following example, the hi-hat is opened on the "+" of "4" and therefore closes on beat "1."

Remember, start working very slowly, be sure to count aloud, and refer to the audio CD for extra help.

Exercise 1 track 34

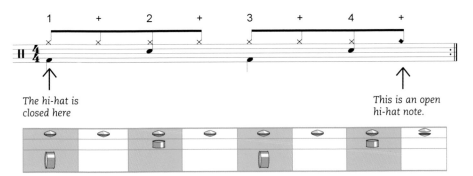

The hi-hat is closed here

This is an open hi-hat note.

Lesson 32:
Eighth-Note Grooves with Open Hi-hat

Exercise 2

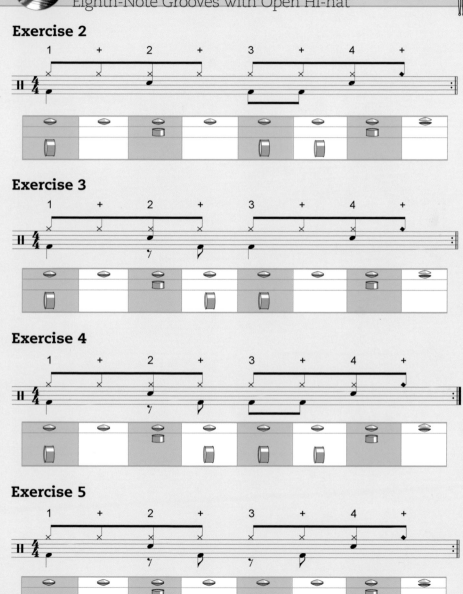

Exercise 3

Exercise 4

Exercise 5

In the following exercises, the hi-hat opens on both the "+" of "2," and the "+" of beat "4." As usual, the hi-hat closes again an eighth-note later, in this case on the "1," and the "3." Only the musical notation and the count are provided.

Exercise 6

Exercise 7

Exercise 8

Exercise 9

Exercise 10

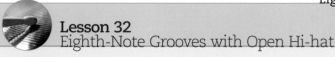

Lesson 32
Eighth-Note Grooves with Open Hi-hat

In the following exercises, the hi-hat is opened on the "+" of "1," and the "+" of "3." Notice how this affects the sound of the groove.

Here, only the musical notation is provided.

Exercise 11

Exercise 12

Exercise 13

Exercise 14

Exercise 15

33 Eighth-Note Grooves with Sixteenth-Note Snare Drum Variations 1

On the CD
Tracks 35–36

Want to read music?
See Reading and
Notation page 38.

So far, all of the snare drum variations that you have played have been based on the addition of eighth-notes in the snare drum part. Now, you will continue to develop your 3-way coordination by looking at snare drum variations involving sixteenth-notes.

The following exercises involve the addition of an extra snare drum note on the "a" of beat "2." Because you are now playing sixteenth-notes, notice that the count has changed. Start by slowly counting "1 e + a 2 e + a 3 e + a 4 e + a," out aloud, over and over, making sure all the counts are even. Next, using the right hand play a hi-hat note on each of the beats (counts "1," "2," "3," and "4"), and each of the "+"s. Notice that although you are also counting the "e"s and the "a"s for the time being, you are not playing them. Next, add the backbeat by playing the snare drum on beats "2" and "4." Finally, add in the extra snare drum note on the "a" of "2." The extra snare drum note comes in between the hi-hat notes.

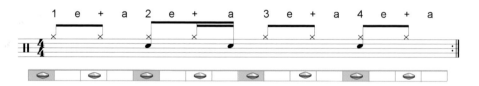

Once you are comfortable playing the hi-hat and snare drum part while counting aloud, it is time to try the following exercises. Remember to check out the audio examples on the CD for reference.

Exercise 1 track 35

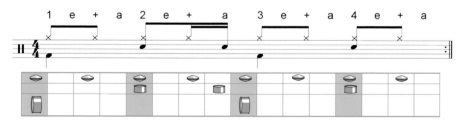

Lesson 33:
Eighth-Note Grooves with Sixteenth-Note
Snare Drum Variations 1

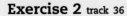

Exercise 2 track 36

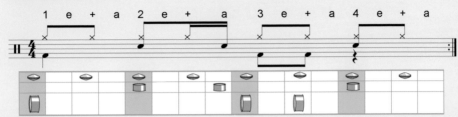

Exercise 3

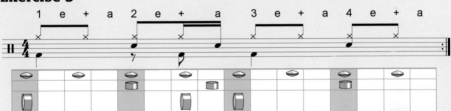

Exercise 4

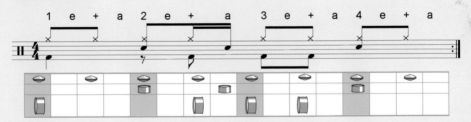

Exercise 5

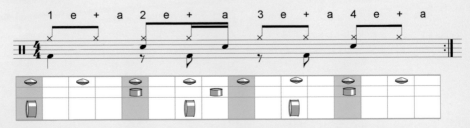

34 Eighth-Note Grooves with Sixteenth-Note Snare Drum Variations 2

On the CD
Tracks 37–38

Want to read music?
See Reading and
Notation page 38.

Continuing on from the previous lesson, you will now look at another common sixteenth-note snare drum variation. This time the extra note is played on the "e" of "3." The hi-hat and snare drum are written below.

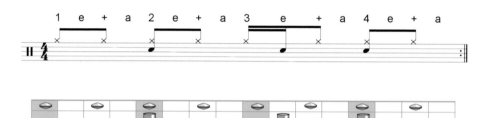

When learning a new pattern such as this one, it is very important to work slowly and count all of the sixteenth-notes out aloud. Make sure that you are comfortable playing the hi-hat and snare drum part before adding the bass drum, and don't forget to refer to the audio examples on the CD.

Exercise 1 track 37

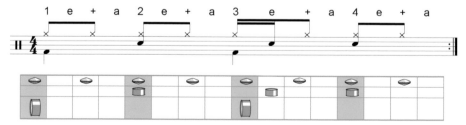

Lesson 34:
Eighth-Note Grooves with Sixteenth-Note
Snare Drum Variations 2

Exercise 2 track 38

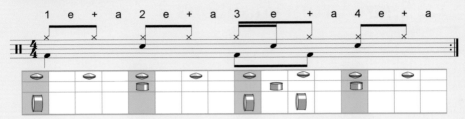

Exercise 3

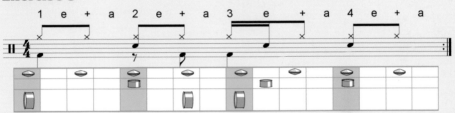

Exercise 4

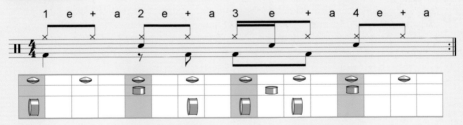

Exercise 5

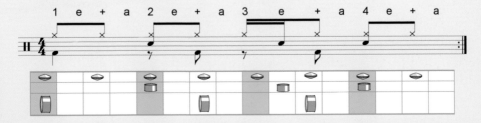

35 Eighth-Note Grooves with Sixteenth-Note Snare Drum Variations 3

On the CD
Tracks 39–40

Want to read music?
See Reading and
Notation page 38.

By now you should be playing some pretty funky-sounding grooves!

In this lesson, you will conclude your study of sixteenth-note snare drum variations by looking at grooves that involve both of the previous two variations. In other words, you will be playing an extra snare drum note on the "a" of "2" and the "e" of "3." The hi-hat and snare drum part are shown below. Notice that only the musical notation and the count are given.

As always, get comfortable with the hi-hat and snare drum parts before moving on. This means starting slowly and continuing to count aloud using the examples on the audio CD for reference.

Lesson 35:
Eighth-Note Grooves with Sixteenth-Note
Snare Drum Variations 3

Exercise 1 track 39

Exercise 2 track 40

Exercise 3

Exercise 4

Exercise 5

36 Eighth-Note Grooves with Sixteenth-Note Bass Drum Patterns 1

On the CD
Track 41

Want to read music?
See Reading and
Notation page 38.

Although you've looked at the use of sixteenth-notes in the snare drum, so far you have only played bass drum patterns featuring eighth notes. The next step in the development of your 3-way coordination is to look at some of the most common sixteenth-note figures that can be played in the bass drum.

The exercises in this lesson incorporate the following sixteenth-note bass-drum figure.

An explanation of this sixteenth-note figure can be found in Lesson 7.

Exercise 1 track 41

1: Start by counting "1 e + a 2 e + a 3 e + a 4 e + a" out aloud, over and over, making sure all the counts are even. Next, using the right hand, play a hi-hat note on each of the beats (counts "1," "2," "3," and "4") and each of the "+"s. Notice that although you are also counting the "e"s and the "a"s, you are not playing them.

2: While still playing the hi-hat, add the bass drum part. In this exercise, you will be playing a bass drum note on every count of "1" and every count of "3" as well as the "a" of "2." Playing the bass drum in between the hi-hats like this can be a little tricky at first, especially while counting aloud, so work very slowly.

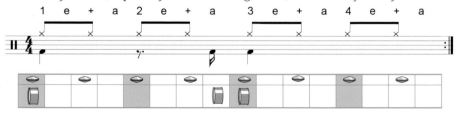

Lesson 36:
Eighth-Note Grooves with Sixteenth-Note
Bass Drum Patterns 1

3: Once you are comfortable with the hi-hat and bass drum part, complete the groove by adding the backbeat.

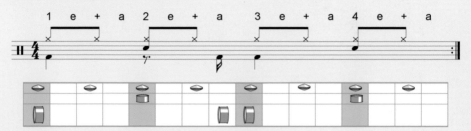

You're now playing grooves involving sixteenth-note bass drum parts. The remaining exercises will help you to continue developing this type of 3-way coordination. Start with the hi-hat part and work through the same process as in the previous lessons.

Exercise 2

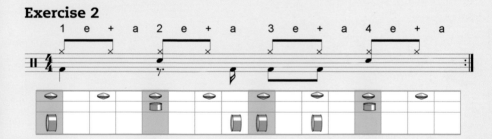

Exercise 3

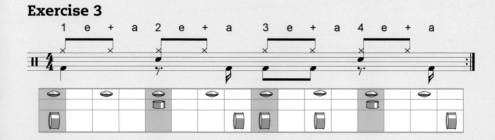

37 *Eighth-Note Grooves with Sixteenth-Note Bass Drum Patterns 2*

On the CD
Track 42

Want to read music?
See Reading and
Notation page 38.

The exercises in this lesson introduce another sixteenth note figure commonly applied to the bass drum:

An explanation of this sixteenth-note figure can be found in Lesson 7.

Exercise 1 track 42

1: Once again, whilst counting aloud start with the hi-hat part:

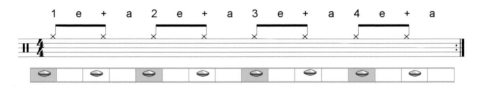

2: Next, add the bass drum. In this exercise the bass drum is played on every count of "1," every count of "3" and the "a" of "3."

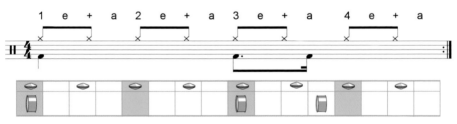

3: Add the backbeat.

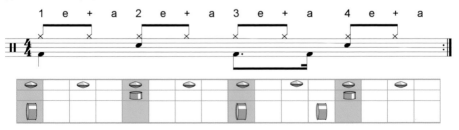

Lesson 37:
Eighth-Note Grooves with Sixteenth-Note
Bass Drum Patterns 2

Using the same process, work slowly through the following exercises.

Exercise 2

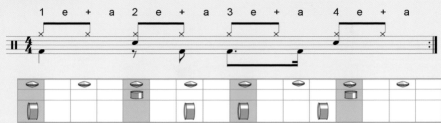

Exercise 3

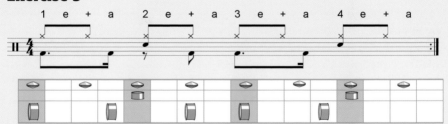

Exercise 4

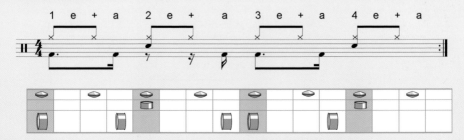

38 *Eighth-Note Grooves with Sixteenth-Note Bass Drum Patterns 3*

On the CD
Track 43

Want to read music?
See Reading and
Notation page 38.

The exercises in this lesson introduce another sixteenth-note figure commonly applied to the bass drum.

An explanation of this sixteenth-note figure can be found in Lesson 7.

Use the same process as in the previous lessons to develop the following grooves.

Exercise 1 track 43

1: Start with the hi-hat.

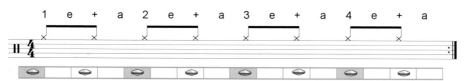

2: Add the bass drum.

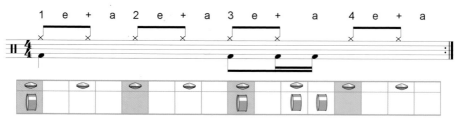

3: Add the snare drum to complete the groove.

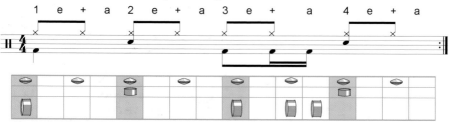

Lesson 38:
Eighth-Note Grooves with Sixteenth-Note
Bass Drum Patterns 3

Exercise 2

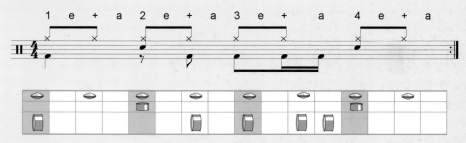

Exercise 3

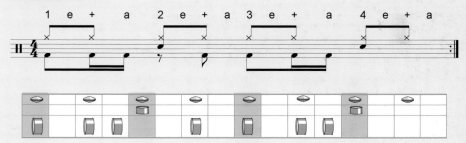

Exercise 4

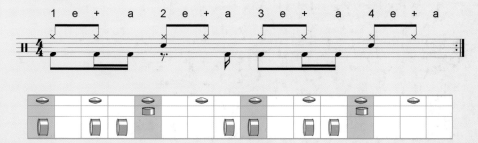

39 Eighth-Note Grooves with Sixteenth-Note Bass Drum Patterns 4

On the CD
Track 44

Want to read music?
See Reading and
Notation page 38.

The grooves in this lesson incorporate the following sixteenth-note figure:

1 e + a

An explanation of this sixteenth-note figure can be found in Lesson 7.

Exercise 1 track 44

1: Start with the hi-hat.

2: Add the bass drum, which is played on every count of "1" as well as the "+" and "a" of beat "3."

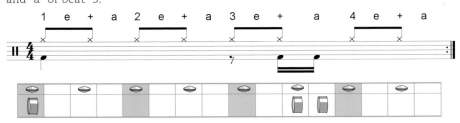

3: Play the snare drum on "2" and "4."

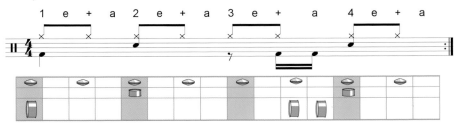

Lesson 39:
Eighth-Note Grooves with Sixteenth-Note
Bass Drum Patterns 4

Continue by applying this process to another groove with a different bass drum pattern.

Exercise 2

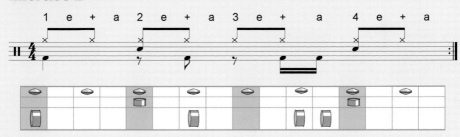

Exercise 3

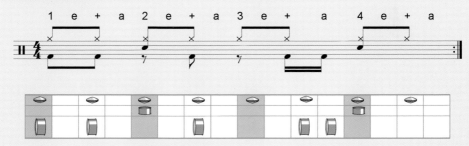

Exercise 4

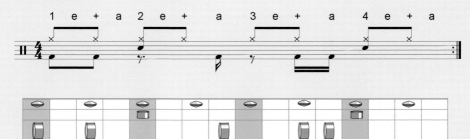

40 Eighth-Note Grooves with Sixteenth-Note Bass Drum Patterns 5

On the CD
Tracks 45–47

Want to read music?
See Reading and
Notation page 38.

You have come a long way since the beginning of this book, and by now you should be able to play some interesting sounding grooves.

In this lesson we will conclude our study of 3-way coordination involving sixteenth-note bass drum patterns, by looking at 10 exercises that combine all of the figures introduced in the previous four lessons. Only the notation and the count are provided here, so don't forget to refer to the examples on the audio CD as necessary.

Exercise 1 track 45

Exercise 2 track 46

Exercise 3 track 47

Exercise 4

Lesson 40:
Eighth-Note Grooves with Sixteenth-Note
Bass Drum Patterns 5

Exercise 5

Exercise 6

Exercise 7

Exercise 8

Exercise 9

Exercise 10

41 Sixteenth-Note Grooves *with* Eighth-Note Bass Drum Patterns

On the CD
Tracks 48-49

Want to read music?
See Reading and
Notation page 38.

It's now time to look at some different hi-hat patterns that can be applied to the grooves that were introduced in previous lessons.

The hi-hat part used here is a sixteenth-note pattern played with both hands. The sequence of right- and left-hand notes (or "sticking") is easy. Simply play one note with each hand: R, L, R, L, R, L, R, L, and so on. In drumming this is known as "single-strokes," or "alternating strokes."

Exercise 1 track 48

Sitting at a drumset with the sticks in your hands and the hi-hat closed, play constant, slow, even notes on the hi-hat using alternating strokes. When you are comfortable with this, add the sixteenth-note counting sequence.

Count, "1 e + a 2 e + a 3 e + a 4 e + a" out aloud over and over, making sure all the counts are even and each count comes with a hi-hat note. The hi-hat part that you are now playing is the basis of all the grooves that you will learn to play in this section.

Written out, it looks like this. Notice that in this case the sticking is written underneath.

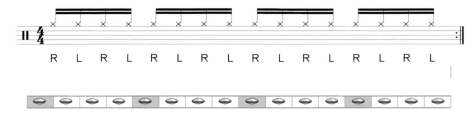

1: While still playing the hi-hat part, play a bass drum note on every count of "1" and every count of "3." This means that the hi-hat and bass drum will be played together on beats "1" and "3." Both bass drum notes fall with the right hand.

Lesson 41:
Sixteenth-Note Grooves with Eighth-Note
Bass Drum Patterns

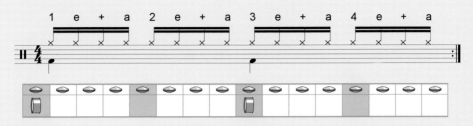

2: Now, add a backbeat. In order to play a snare drum note on every count of "2" and "4," bring the right hand over from the hi-hat to play the snare drum instead. Notice that in this case, when we add the backbeat there is no longer a hi-hat note on beats "2" and "4."

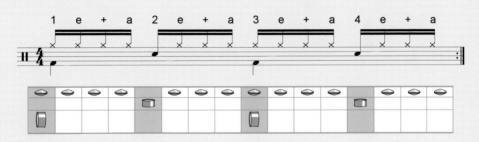

3: Continue by applying this process to another groove with a different bass drum pattern.

Exercise 2 track 49

1: Start with the hi-hat and play the beat below.

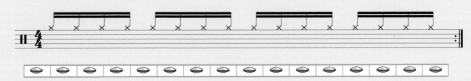

2: Add the bass drum. As in the previous example, you will play bass drum on beats "1" and "3" but in this groove there is an additional bass drum on the "+" of "3." As in the previous example, all bass drum notes fall with the right hand.

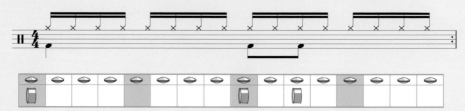

3: Playing the snare drum on "2" and "4" completes the groove. Remember, to do this, you must move the right hand over to the hi-hat.

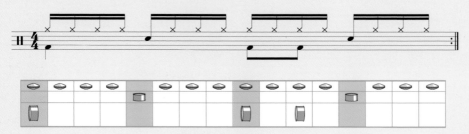

Continue by applying this process to the following grooves.

Exercise 3

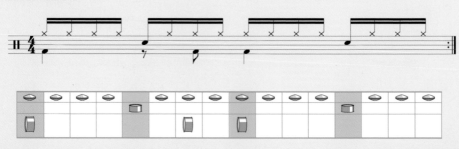

Lesson 41:
Sixteenth-Note Grooves with Eighth-Note
Bass Drum Patterns

Exercise 4

Exercise 5

Exercise 6

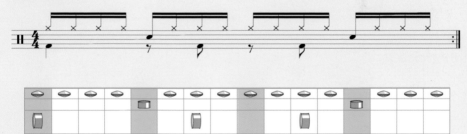

In the following exercises, only the musical notation and count are provided.

Exercise 6

Exercise 7

Exercise 8

Exercise 9

Exercise 10

Lesson 41:
Sixteenth-Note Grooves with Eighth-Note
Bass Drum Patterns

In the following exercises, only the musical notation is provided.

Exercise 11

Exercise 12

Exercise 13

Exercise 14

Exercise 15

42 Sixteenth-Note Grooves *with* Sixteenth-Note Snare Drum Variations 1

On the CD
Track 50

Want to read music?
See Reading and
Notation page 38.

Now, you will continue to develop these sixteenth-note grooves by looking at snare drum variations involving sixteenth-notes.

The following exercises involve the addition of an extra snare drum note on the "a" of beat "2." As the hi-hat part is being played with both hands, this involves moving the left hand over from the hi-hat to play the extra snare drum note.

The hi-hat and snare drum part that you are now playing is the basis of all the grooves that you will learn to play in this section. Written out, it looks like this. Notice that in this case the sticking is written underneath.

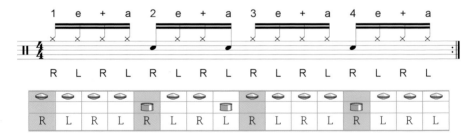

Once you are comfortable playing the hi-hat and snare drum part while counting aloud, try the following exercises.

Exercise 1 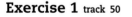track 50

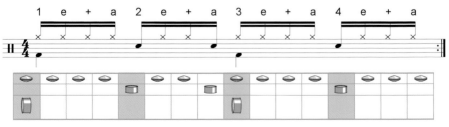

Lesson 42:
Sixteenth-Note Grooves with Sixteenth-Note
Snare Drum Variations 1

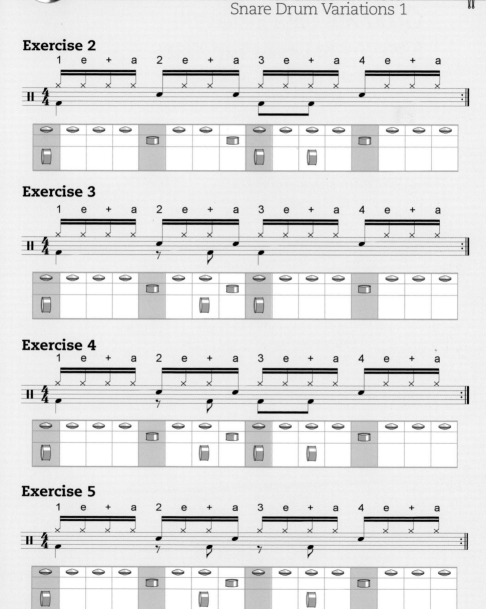

43 Sixteenth-Note Grooves with Sixteenth-Note Snare Drum Variations 2

On the CD
Track 51

Want to read music?
See Reading and
Notation page 38.

Continuing on from the previous lesson, you will now look at another common sixteenth-note snare drum variation. This time the extra note is played on the "e" of "3." The hi-hat and snare drum are written below. Again, the left hand comes over from the hi-hat to play the extra snare drum note.

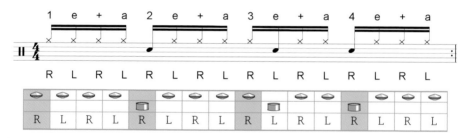

As you know by now, when learning a new pattern such as this one it is very important to work slowly and count all of the sixteenth-notes aloud. Make sure that you are comfortable playing the hi-hat and snare drum part, before adding the bass drum.

Exercise 1 track 51

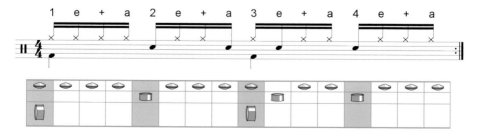

Lesson 43:
Sixteenth-Note Grooves with Sixteenth-Note
Snare Drum Variations 2

Exercise 2

Exercise 3

Exercise 4

Exercise 5

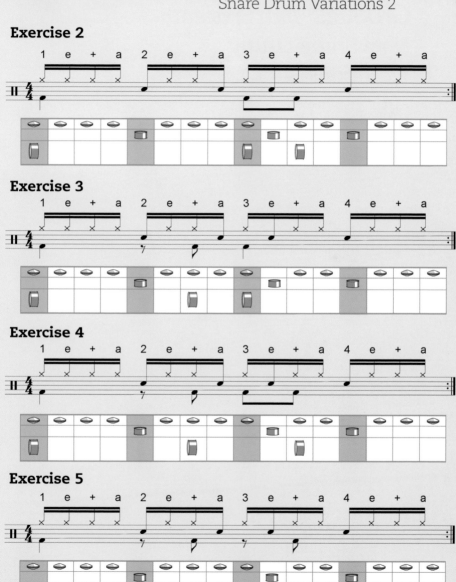

44 Sixteenth-Note Grooves with Sixteenth-Note Snare Drum Variations 3

On the CD
Track 52

Want to read music?
See Reading and
Notation page 38.

In this lesson you will conclude your study of sixteenth-note snare drum variations by looking at grooves that involve both of the previous two variations. In other words, you will play an extra snare drum note on the "a" of "2" and the "e" of "3." The hi-hat and snare drum part are shown below.

As in the previous lessons, the left-hand is responsible for playing the extra snare drum notes. Notice that only the musical notation and the count are given.

Exercise 1 track 52

Lesson 44:
Sixteenth-Note Grooves with Sixteenth-Note
Snare Drum Variations 3

Exercise 2

Exercise 3

Exercise 4

Exercise 5

On the CD
Tracks 53

Want to read music?
See Reading and
Notation page 38.

45 Sixteenth-Note Grooves with Sixteenth-Note Bass Drum Patterns 1

Although you have looked at the use of sixteenth-notes in the snare drum, so far you have only played bass drum patterns featuring eighth-notes. The next step in the development of these sixteenth-note grooves is to look at some of the sixteenth-note figures that can be played on the bass drum.

The exercises here incorporate the following sixteenth-note bass drum figure.

1 e + a

An explanation of this sixteenth-note figure can be found in Lesson 7.

Exercise 1 track 53

Sitting at the drums with the sticks in your hands and the hi-hat closed, play constant, slow, even notes on the hi-hat using alternating strokes. When you are comfortable with this, add the sixteenth-note counting sequence.

Count "1 e + a 2 e + a 3 e + a 4 e + a," out aloud over and over, making sure all the counts are even and each count comes with a hi-hat note. The hi-hat part that you are now playing is the basis of all the grooves that you'll learn to play here.

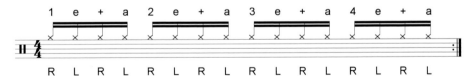

Written out, it looks like the table below. Notice that in this case the sticking is written underneath.

Lesson 45:
Sixteenth-Note Grooves with Sixteenth-Note
Bass Drum Patterns 1

While still playing the hi-hat part, add the bass drum part. In this exercise, you will be playing a bass drum note on every count of "1," every count of "3" as well as the "a" of "2." Notice that the bass drum note on the "a" of "2" falls with a left-hand hi-hat. Playing these unisons between the left hand and the right foot can be tricky at first, so work very slowly and concentrate on accurate execution.

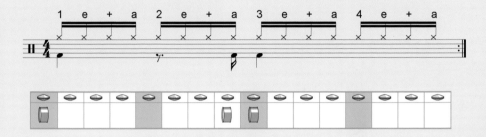

Once you are comfortable with the hi-hat and bass drum part, complete the groove by adding the backbeat.

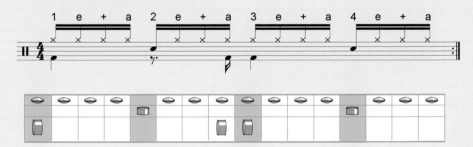

The exercises over the page will help you to continue developing this type of 3-way coordination. Start with the hi-hat part and work through the same process as in the previous lessons.

Lesson 45:
Sixteenth-Note Grooves with Sixteenth-Note
Bass Drum Patterns 1

Exercise 2

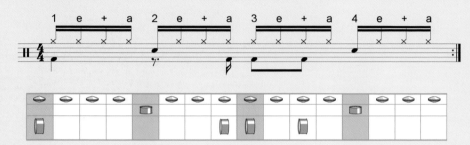

Exercise 3

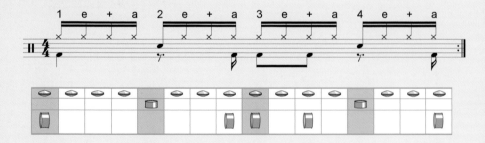

Exercise 4

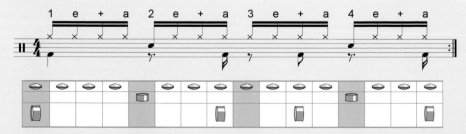

On the CD
Track 54

Want to read music?
See Reading and
Notation page 38.

Sixteenth-Note 46
Grooves *with*
Sixteenth-Note
Bass Drum Patterns 2

These exercises introduce another sixteenth-note figure
commonly applied to the bass drum.

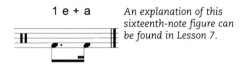

1 e + a

An explanation of this
sixteenth-note figure can
be found in Lesson 7.

Exercise 1 track 54

1: Once again, while counting aloud, start with the hi-hat part.

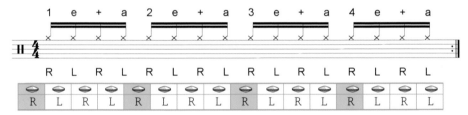

2: While still playing the hi-hat part, add the bass drum part. In this exercise,
you will be playing a bass drum note on every count of "1" and every count of "3"
as well as the "a" of "3." As in the previous lesson, pay attention to the unisons
between the hi-hat and the bass drum.

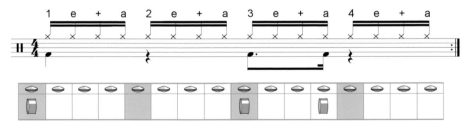

Lesson 46:
Sixteenth-Note Grooves with Sixteenth-Note
Bass Drum Patterns 2

3: Once you are comfortable with the hi-hat and bass drum part, complete the groove by adding the backbeat.

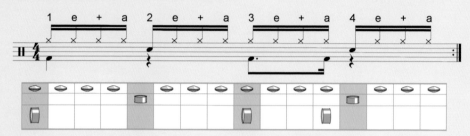

Using the same process, work slowly through the following exercises.

Exercise 2

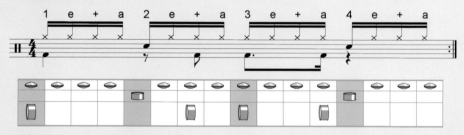

Exercise 3

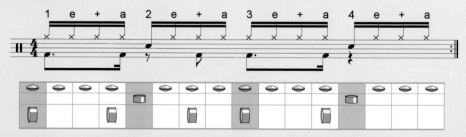

**On the CD
Track 55**

Want to read music?
See Reading and
Notation page 38.

Sixteenth-Note 47
Grooves *with*
Sixteenth-Note
Bass Drum Patterns 3

In this lesson the following sixteenth-note figure is introduced.

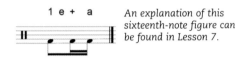

1 e + a

*An explanation of this
sixteenth-note figure can
be found in Lesson 7.*

Use the same process as in the previous lessons to develop the following grooves.

Exercise 1 track 55

1: Start with the hi-hat, below.

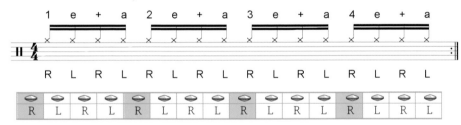

2: While still playing the hi-hat part, add the bass drum part. In this exercise, you will be playing a bass drum note on every count of "1" and every count of "3" as well as the "+" and "a" of "3." As in the previous lesson, pay attention to the unisons between the hi-hat and the bass drum.

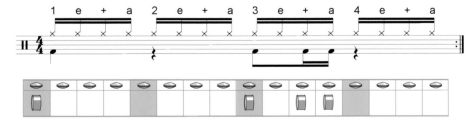

Lesson 47:
Sixteenth-Note Grooves with Sixteenth-Note Bass Drum Patterns 3

3: Add the snare drum to complete the groove.

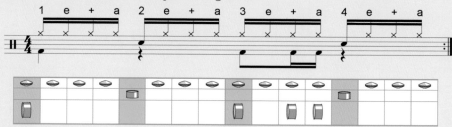

Exercise 2

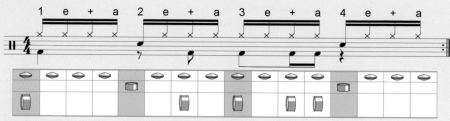

Exercise 3

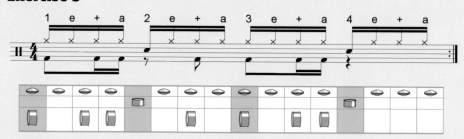

Exercise 4

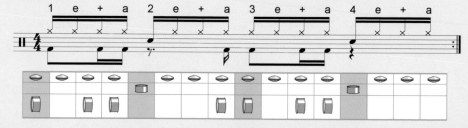

On the CD
Track 56

Want to read music?
See Reading and
Notation page 38.

Sixteenth-Note 48
Grooves *with*
Sixteenth-Note
Bass Drum Patterns 4

*The grooves in this lesson incorporate the following
sixteenth-note figure.*

*An explanation of this
sixteenth-note figure can
be found in Lesson 7.*

Exercise 1 track 56
1: Start with the hi-hat, below.

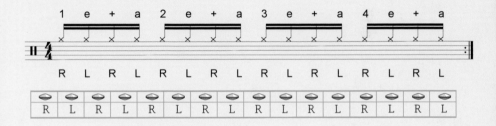

2: While still playing the hi-hat part, add the bass drum part. In this exercise, you
will be playing a bass drum note on every count of "1," as well as the "+" and the
"a" of "3." As in the previous lesson, pay attention to the unisons between the hi-
hat and the bass drum.

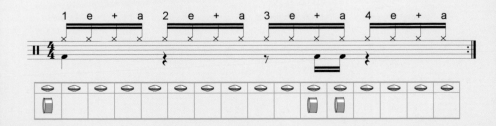

Lesson 48:
Sixteenth-Note Grooves with Sixteenth-Note
Bass Drum Patterns 4

3: Once you are comfortable with the hi-hat and bass drum part, complete the groove by adding the backbeat.

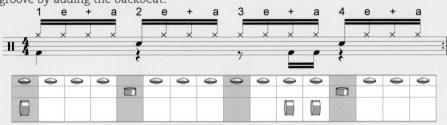

Continue by applying the same process to the following exercises.

Exercise 2 track 57

Exercise 3

Exercise 4

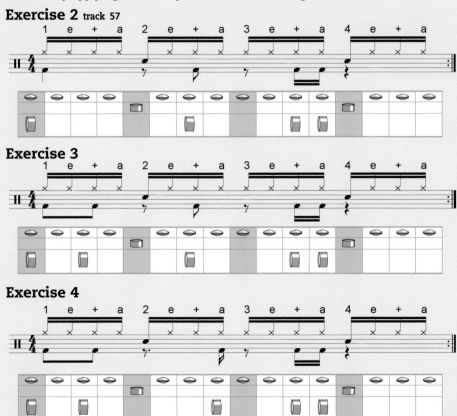

On the CD
Tracks 58–60

Want to read music?
See Reading and
Notation page 38.

Sixteenth-Note 49 Grooves *with* Sixteenth-Note Bass Drum Patterns 5

This lesson will conclude the study of sixteenth-note grooves involving sixteenth-note bass drum patterns by looking at ten exercises that combine all of the figures introduced in the previous four lessons.

Only the notation and the count are provided here, so do not forget to refer to the examples on the audio CD as necessary.

Exercise 1 track 58

Exercise 2 track 59

Exercise 3 track 60

Exercise 4

Exercise 5

Exercise 6

Exercise 7

Lesson 49:
Sixteenth-Note Grooves with Sixteenth-Note
Bass Drum Patterns 5

Exercise 8

Exercise 9

Exercise 10

50 Other Right-Hand Ostinatos

On the CD
Tracks 61–63

Want to read music?
See Reading and
Notation page 38.

So far, you have looked at grooves featuring two different right-hand hi-hat patterns: eighth-notes in the right hand, which is shown again in Exercise 1, and sixteenth-notes played with both hands, which is shown again in Exercise 2.

As you continue developing your coordination, consider other right-hand ostinatos. In this lesson you will look at some of those most commonly used today. All of the examples here are written on the hi-hat but remember that they can all be transposed to the ride cymbal.

What's an Ostinato?

An Ostinato is a short musical pattern that is repeated constantly throughout a song or section of a song.

Exercise 1

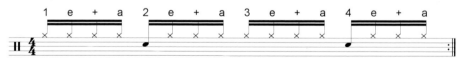

Exercise 2

Exercise 3

Here you see simple straight quarter-notes. Although this pattern works well at a variety of tempos, it sounds particularly effective when played at quicker speeds, especially when played on the bell of the ride cymbal.

Lesson 50:
Other Right-Hand Ostinatos

Exercise 4 track 61

Here is the previous pattern written out with a simple bass drum and snare drum part.

Exercise 5

Here you see "upbeat" eighth-notes. Effective at a variety of tempos, it has a syncopated, funky sound.

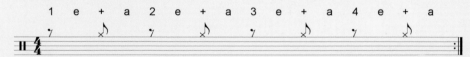

Exercise 6 track 62

This is the previous pattern, written out with a simple bass and snare drum part.

Exercise 7

Here you see sixteenth-notes once again, but this time they should all be played with the right hand. Naturally, it is not possible to play this type of pattern as quickly with only one hand so it works better at medium tempos. However, when mastered it has a "smoother" feel than the two-handed version making it sound funkier.

Exercise 8 track 63

This is the previous pattern, written out with a simple bass and snare drum part.

51 *Eighth-Note Grooves with Eighth-Note Bass Drum Patterns*

On the CD
Tracks 64–65
Want to read music?
See Reading and
Notation page 38.

All of the coordination exercises so far have involved the use of the hi-hat (played with the right hand), the snare drum (played with the left hand) and the bass drum (played with the right foot).

Although the left foot wasn't actually playing anything during the previous exercises, it had the important job of keeping the hi-hat closed. The left foot, in other words, is responsible for controlling the sound of the hi-hat. This is important to remember because sometimes, in order to get a different sound, drummers will move the right-hand from the hi-hat and play it on the ride cymbal. When this is done, the left foot no longer controls the sound of the hi-hat because it isn't being played.

This means that the drummer can use the left foot to play another pattern along with the ride cymbal, snare drum and bass drum. The following exercises will help you develop this type of coordination.

The parts of the drum set you will be using are the:

- **Ride cymbal**
  Played with the right hand
- **Snare drum**
  Played with the left hand
- **Bass drum**
  Played with the right foot
- **Hi-hat**
  Played with the left foot

Because playing these patterns involves the use of four limbs, drummers call this type of coordination "4-way coordination."

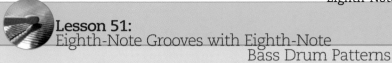

Lesson 51:
Eighth-Note Grooves with Eighth-Note
Bass Drum Patterns

Exercise 1 track 64

1: Below is the pattern that you will play on the hi-hat with the left foot. Because you are playing the hi-hat with the foot, and not the hand, the notes are written lower down the staff below the first line. Even though the hi-hat only comes on beats "1, 2, 3," and "4" it is important to count all of the eighth-notes aloud while playing this pattern.

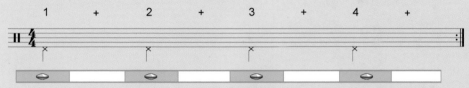

2: Add the bass drum. In this case, play it on beats "1" and "3," which means that each bass drum note comes with a hi-hat note. When you play two notes together like this it is described as being in unison.

Make sure that you continue to count aloud while playing this pattern.

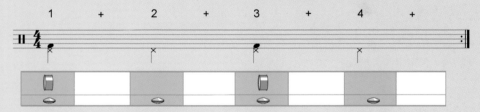

3: The next stage is to add the ride cymbal. Because you are playing eighth-notes here, note that the ride cymbal comes on every count.

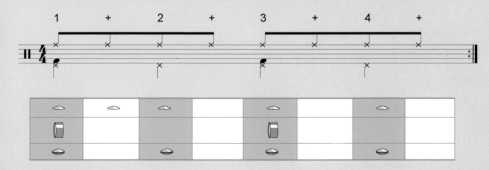

4: Add the backbeat. As you know by now, the backbeat is when the snare drum is played on beats "2" and "4." Continue counting aloud.

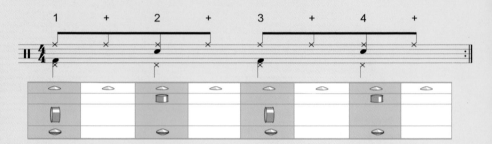

Exercise 2 track 65

Now go through this process again, this time using a different bass drum pattern.
1: Once again, start with just the hi-hat.

2: Next, add the bass drum. Notice the extra bass drum note here on the "+" of "3."

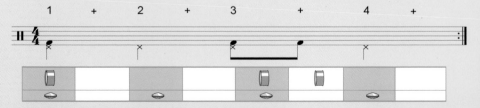

Lesson 51:
Eighth-Note Grooves with Eighth-Note
Bass Drum Patterns

3: Once again, the ride cymbal is next.

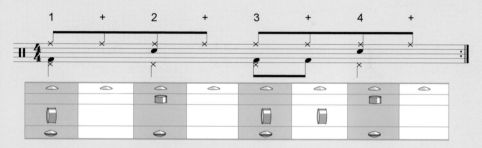

4: And finally, complete our groove by adding the backbeat in the snare drum.

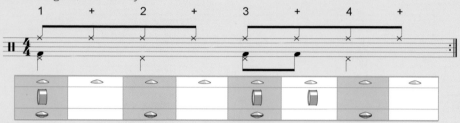

Now that you understand how to develop these types of grooves, use the same process to learn to play the following grooves.

Exercise 3

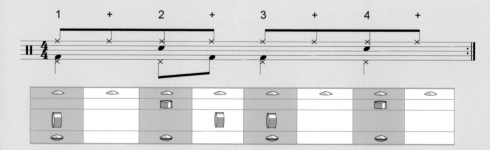

Exercise 4

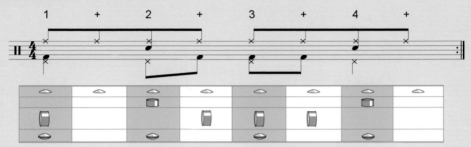

Exercise 5

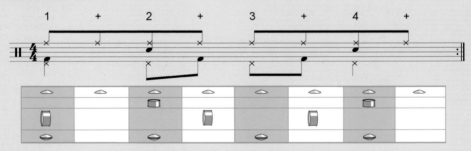

In the following examples, only the musical notation and the count are given.

Exercise 6

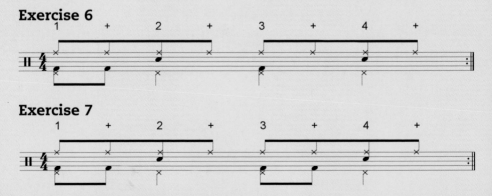

Exercise 7

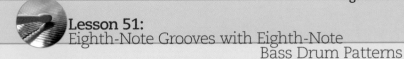

Lesson 51:
Eighth-Note Grooves with Eighth-Note
Bass Drum Patterns

Exercise 8

Exercise 9

Exercise 10

In the following exercises only the musical notation is given.

Exercise 11

Exercise 12

Did you notice that the bass drum patterns used here are the same ones that were introduced previously in the 3-way coordination?

When you are comfortable with these grooves individually, practice playing each one four times before moving on to the next without stopping

52 *Eighth-Note Grooves with Eighth-Note Snare Drum Variations*

Want to read music?
See Reading and
Notation page 38.

In the previous lesson you began developing your 4-way coordination by playing different bass drum figures against a constant ride, hi-hat and snare drum pattern. In this lesson you will continue developing your coordination, this time by playing different figures in the snare drum.

The following exercises feature the same bass drum patterns as those in the previous lesson but an extra snare drum is added on the "+" of "4." Consequently, the ride, hi-hat and snare drum part looks like this.

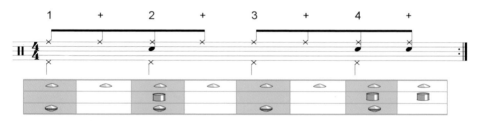

Start working very slowly and don't forget to count aloud. Make sure that you are comfortable playing the hi-hat and snare drum part before moving on.

Exercise 1

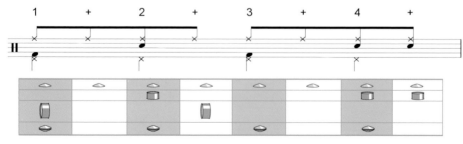

Lesson 52:
Eighth-Note Grooves with Eighth-Note
Snare Drum Variations

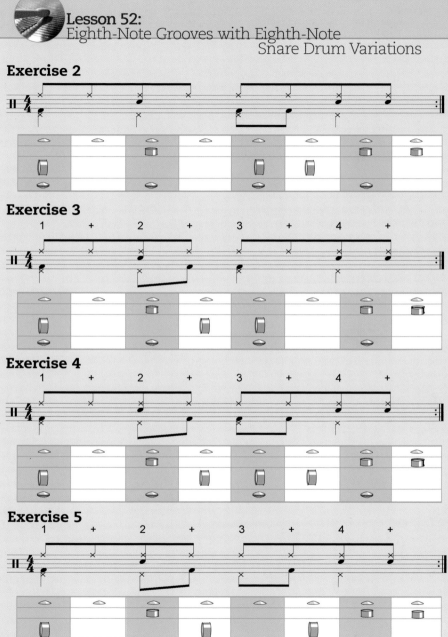

Lesson 52:
Eighth-Note Grooves with Eighth-Note Snare Drum Variations

Here, you are no longer playing an extra snare drum note on the "+" of "4" but instead on the "+" of "1." Notice how this affects the feel of these grooves.

In these exercises, only the musical notation and the count are provided.

Exercise 6

Exercise 7

Exercise 8

Exercise 9

Exercise 10

Eighth-Note Grooves 53
with Sixteenth-Note
Snare Drum Variations 1

Want to read music?
See Reading and
Notation page 38.

*So far, all of the snare drum variations that you have played,
have been based on the addition of eighth-notes in the snare
drum part. Now, you will continue to develop your 4-way
coordination by looking at snare drum variations involving
sixteenth-notes.*

These exercises involve an extra snare drum note on the "a" of beat "2." Because
you are now playing sixteenth-notes, notice that the count has changed.

Start by slowly counting "1 e + a 2 e + a 3 e + a 4 e + a" out aloud, over and over,
making sure all the counts are even. Next, using the right hand, play a ride-note
on each of the beats (counts "1," "2," "3," and "4") and each of the "+"s. Note that
although you are also counting the "e"s, and the "a"s for the time being, you are not
playing them. Next, add the hi-hat on each of the beats. Finally, add the backbeat
by playing the snare drum on beats "2" and "4." Continue counting aloud.

When you are comfortable playing the ride, hi-hat and snare while counting
sixteenth-notes, add in the extra snare drum note on the "a" of "2." You will notice
that the extra snare drum note comes in between the ride cymbal notes.

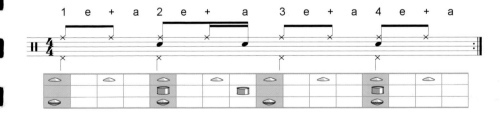

Once you are comfortable playing the hi-hat and snare drum part while counting
aloud, try the exercises over the page.

Exercise 1

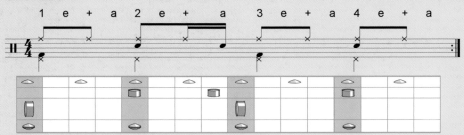

Exercise 2

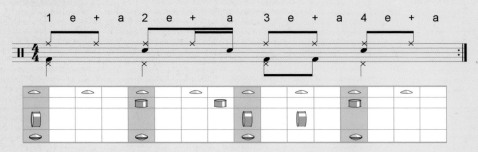

Exercise 3

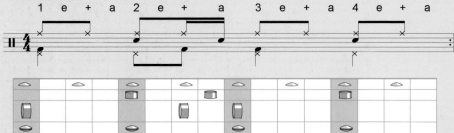

Lesson 53:
Eighth-Note Grooves with Sixteenth-Note
Snare Drum Variations 1

Exercise 4

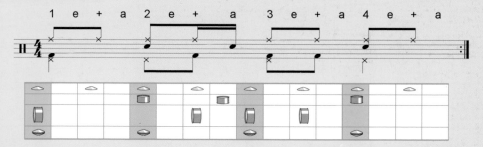

Exercise 5

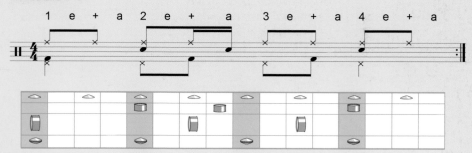

54 *Eighth-Note Grooves with Sixteenth-Note Snare Drum Variations 2*

Want to read music?
See Reading and
Notation page 38.

Continuing from the previous lesson, you will now look at another common sixteenth-note snare drum variation. This time the extra note is played on the "e" of "3." The ride, hi-hat, and snare drum are written below.

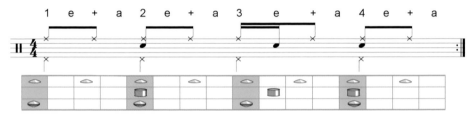

As you know by now, when learning a new pattern such as this one it is very important to work slowly and count all of the sixteenth-notes aloud. Make sure that you are comfortable playing the ride, hi-hat, and snare drum part before adding the bass drum.

Exercise 1

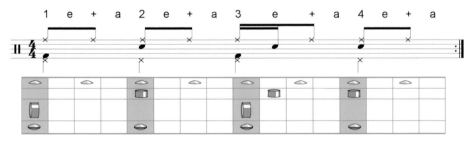

Exercise 2

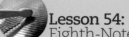

Lesson 54:
Eighth-Note Grooves with Sixteenth-Note
Snare Drum Variations 2

Exercise 3

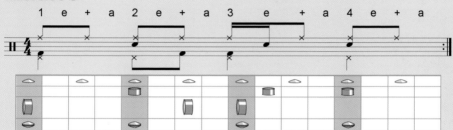

Exercise 4

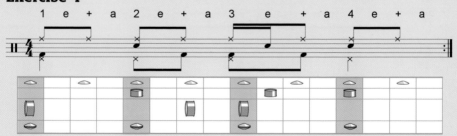

Exercise 5

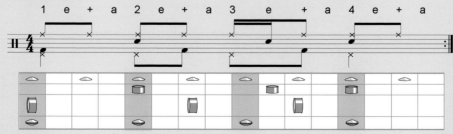

Lesson 54:
Eighth-Note Grooves with Sixteenth-Note
Snare Drum Variations 2

Exercise 6

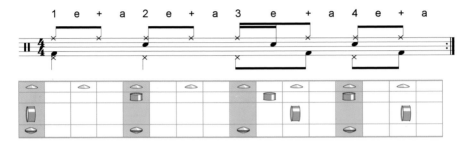

Exercise 7

Exercise 8

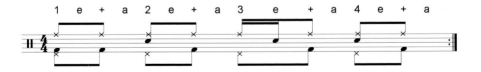

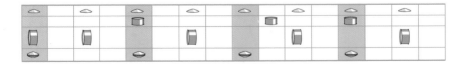

Eighth-Note Grooves 55
with Sixteenth-Note
Snare Drum Variations 3

Want to read music?
See Reading and
Notation page 38.

*Here you will conclude your study of sixteenth-note
snare drum variations by looking at grooves that
involve both of the previous two variations. In other
words, you will be playing an extra snare drum note
on the "a" of "2," and the "e" of "3." The ride, hi-hat,
and snare drum part are shown below. Notice that
only the musical notation is given.*

As always, get very comfortable with the hi-hat and snare drum parts before
moving on. This means starting very slowly, and continuing to count aloud.

Lesson 55:
Eighth-Note Grooves with Sixteenth-Note
Snare Drum Variations 3

Exercise 1

Exercise 2

Exercise 3

Exercise 4

Exercise 5

Eighth-Note Grooves 56
with Sixteenth-Note
Bass Drum Patterns 1

Want to read music?
See Reading and
Notation page 38.

Although you have looked at the use of sixteenth-notes in the snare drum, so far you have only played bass drum patterns featuring eighth-notes. The next step in the development of your 4-way coordination is to look at some of the most common sixteenth-note figures that can be played on the bass drum.

The exercises here incorporate the following sixteenth-note bass drum figure:

1 e + a

An explanation of this sixteenth-note figure can be found in Lesson 7.

Exercise 1

1: Start by slowly counting "1 e + a 2 e + a 3 e + a 4 e + a," aloud, over and over, making sure all the counts are even. Next, using the left foot, play a hi-hat note on each of the beats (counts "1," "2," "3," and "4"). When comfortable, add the bass drum, continuing to count aloud.

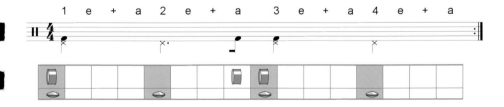

2: Using the right hand, play a ride cymbal note on each of the beats (counts "1," "2," "3," and "4"), and each of the "+"s.

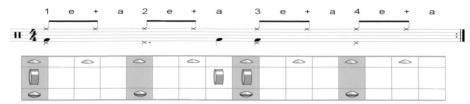

3: Complete the pattern and add the backbeat by playing the snare drum on beats "2" and "4."

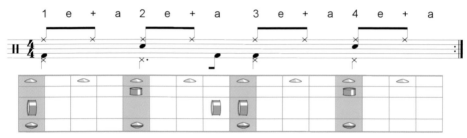

Now continue by applying the same process to a different bass drum pattern.

Exercise 2

1: Start with the hi-hat and bass drum.

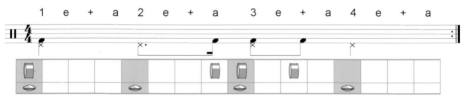

2: Now add the ride.

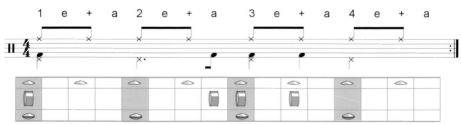

Lesson 56:
Eighth-Note Grooves with Sixteenth-Note
Bass Drum Patterns 1

3: Complete the pattern by adding the backbeat.

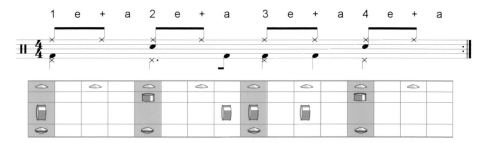

Apply this process to the following grooves below.

Exercise 3

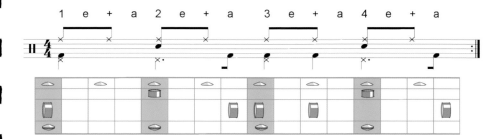

Exercise 4

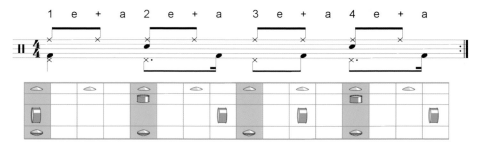

57 Eighth-Note Grooves with Sixteenth-Note Bass Drum Patterns 2

Want to read music?
See Reading and
Notation page 38.

These exercises introduce another sixteenth-note figure commonly applied to the bass drum.

1 e + a

An explanation of this sixteenth-note figure can be found in Lesson 7.

Exercise 1

1: Once again, start with the hi-hat and bass drum.

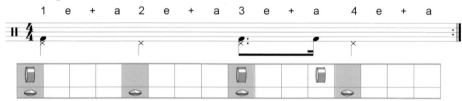

2: Add the ride.

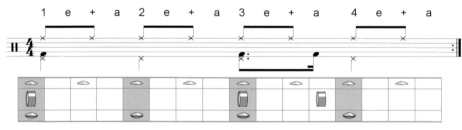

3: Add the backbeat.

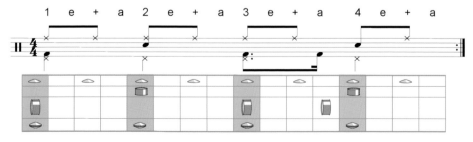

Lesson 57:
Eighth-Note Grooves with Sixteenth-Note
Bass Drum Patterns 2

Now continue by applying this process to a different bass drum pattern.

Exercise 2

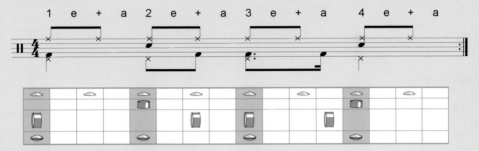

Exercise 3

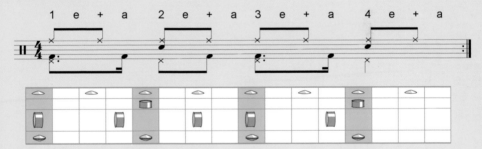

Exercise 4

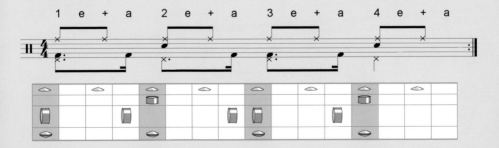

58 Eighth-Note Grooves with Sixteenth-Note Bass Drum Patterns 3

Want to read music?
See Reading and
Notation page 38.

In this lesson the following sixteenth-note figure is introduced.

An explanation of this sixteenth-note figure can be found in Lesson 7.

Use the same process as in the previous lessons to develop the following grooves.

Exercise 1

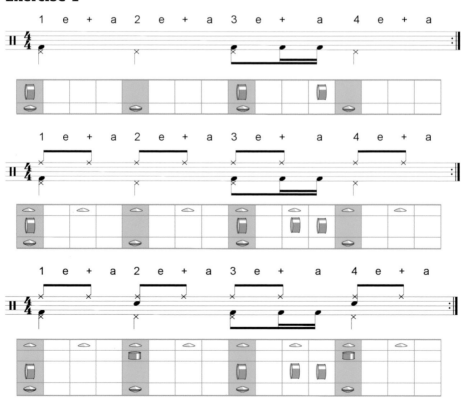

Lesson 58:
Eighth-Note Grooves with Sixteenth-Note
Bass Drum Patterns 3

Exercise 2

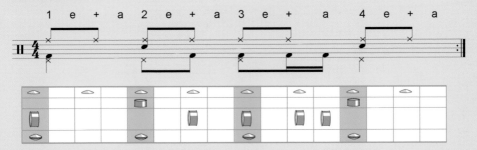

Exercise 3

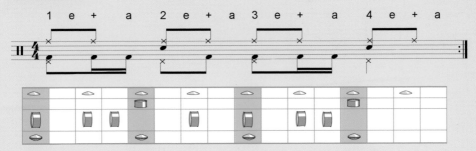

Exercise 4

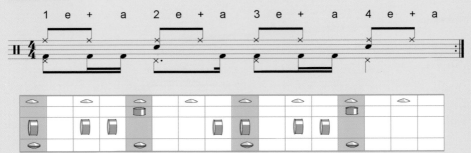

59 Eighth-Note Grooves with Sixteenth-Note Bass Drum Patterns 4

Want to read music?
See Reading and
Notation page 38.

The grooves in this lesson incorporate the following sixteenth-note figure.

1 e + a

An explanation of this sixteenth-note figure can be found in Lesson 7.

Exercise 1

1: Start with hi-hat and bass drum, as below.

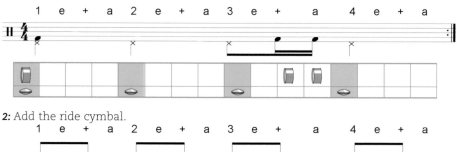

2: Add the ride cymbal.

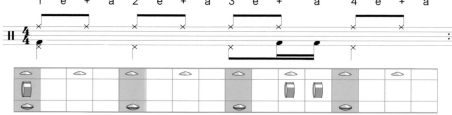

3: Complete the pattern by adding the backbeat.

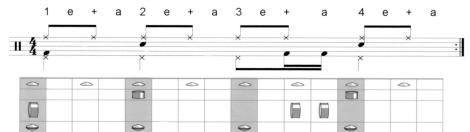

Lesson 59:
Eighth-Note Grooves with Sixteenth-Note
Bass Drum Patterns 4

Exercise 2

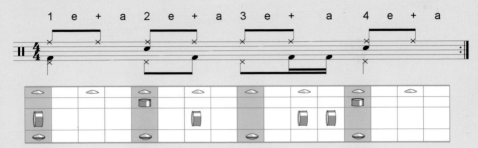

Exercise 3

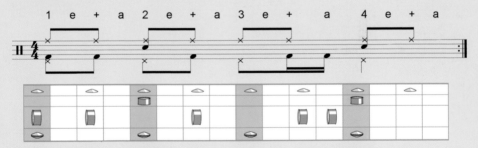

Exercise 4

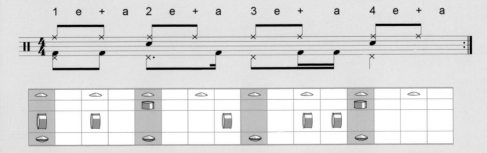

60 *Eighth-Note Grooves with Sixteenth-Note Bass Drum Patterns 5*

Want to read music? See Reading and Notation page 38.

In this lesson you will conclude your study of 4-way coordination involving sixteenth-note bass drum patterns by looking at 10 exercises that combine all of the figures introduced in the previous four lessons.

Only the notation and the count are provided here.

Exercise 1

Exercise 2

Exercise 3

Exercise 4

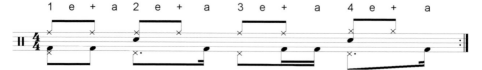

Lesson 60:
Eighth-Note Grooves with Sixteenth-Note
Bass Drum Patterns 5

Exercise 5

Exercise 6

Exercise 7

Exercise 8

Exercise 9

Exercise 10

61 Other Left-Foot Ostinatos

So far, all of the 4-way grooves have featured the same left-foot ostinato. This pattern is shown again in Exercise 1.

Want to read music?
See Reading and
Notation page 38.

Consider other left-foot ostinatos. In this lesson, you will look at some of those most commonly used today.

Exercise 1
Here you see eighth-notes. This is a very common pattern, which has a more "driving" feel than quarter-notes.

Exercise 2
Here is the previous pattern written out with a simple ride, bass drum, and snare drum part.

Exercise 3
Here you see "upbeat" eighth-notes. This pattern has a syncopated, funky sound.

Exercise 4
Here is the previous pattern written out with a simple ride, bass drum, and snare drum part.

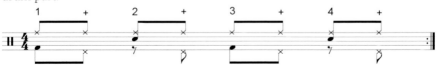

Take the time to review the exercises presented in Lessons 51–60 using these different left-foot patterns. Combine them with your favorite right-hand ostinatos from Lesson 50.

On the CD
Track 66

Want to read music?
See Reading and
Notation page 38.

Eighth-Note Triplet Grooves 62

So far, all of the grooves that you have played have been based on eighth-notes and sixteenth-notes—so, they have an underlying two, or four, feel.

The next step in the development of your coordination is to look at grooves based on an underlying three feel. In this lesson, all of the grooves that we will study are in 4/4 and based on triplets. A full explanation of triplets can be found in Lesson 10.

The parts of the drum set you will be using are the:

Hi-hat
Played with the right hand
Snare drum
Played with the left hand
Bass drum
Played with the right foot

Exercise 1 track 66

1: Sitting at the drums with the sticks in your hands, start by counting "1 + a 2 + a 3 + a 4 + a," out loud, over and over, making sure all the counts are even.

When you are comfortable with this, play a single hi-hat note on every count with the right-hand.

The hi-hat part that you are now playing is the basis of all the grooves that you will learn to play in this section.

Written out, it looks like the music below.

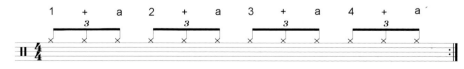

2: While still playing the hi-hat part, play a bass drum note on every count of "1" and every count of "3." This means that the hi-hat and bass drum will be played together on beats "1" and "3."

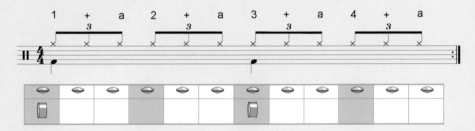

3: Next, while playing the hi-hat and bass drum, play a snare drum note with the left hand on every count of "2" and "4."

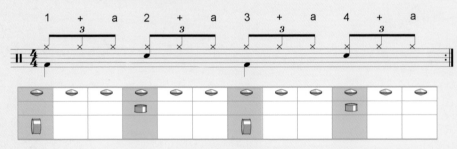

4: Now continue by applying this process to another groove with a different bass drum pattern.

Exercise 2

1: Start with the hi-hat.

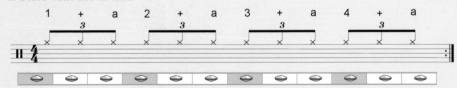

Lesson 62:
Eighth-Note Triplet Grooves

2: Next, add the bass drum. As in the previous example, you will play the bass drum on beats "1" and "3," but in this groove there is an additional bass drum on the "a" of "3."

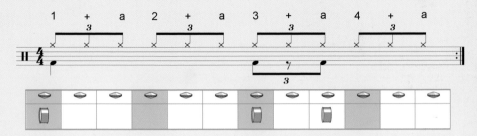

3: Finally, playing the snare drum on "2" and "4" completes the groove.

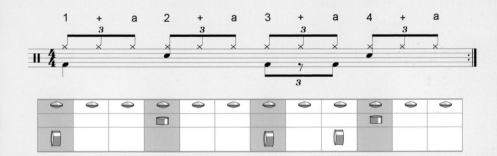

Apply this process to the following grooves.

Exercise 3

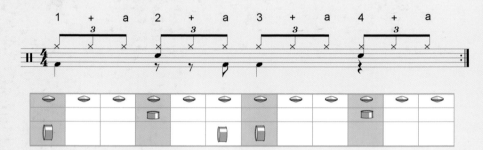

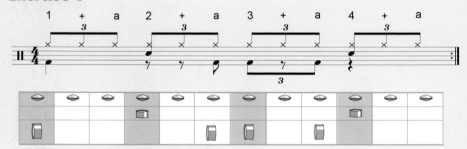

Exercise 4

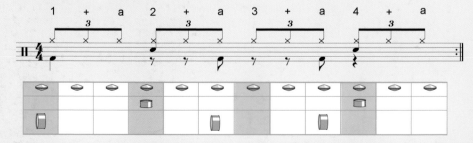

Exercise 5

Lesson 62:
Eighth-Note Triplet Grooves

In the following exercises, only the musical notation and the count are provided.

Exercise 6

Exercise 7

Exercise 8

Exercise 9

Exercise 10

Lesson 62:
Eighth-Note Triplet Grooves

In the following exercises, only the musical notation is provided.

Exercise 11

Exercise 12

Exercise 13

Exercise 14

On the CD
Track 67

Want to read music?
See Reading and
Notation page 38.

Shuffle Grooves 63

The next group of triplet grooves that you will study are called shuffles. Any groove belonging to the shuffle family is characterized by a specific rhythm created by playing the first and third part of the triplet.

Exercise 1 track 67

1: Sitting at the drums with the sticks in your hands, start by slowly counting "1 + a 2 + a 3 + a 4 + a" aloud, over and over, making sure all the counts are even.

When you are comfortable with this, with the right hand play a single hi-hat note on every count of "1," "2," "3," and "4," and every "a."

The hi-hat part that you are now playing is the basis of all shuffle grooves.

Written out, it looks like this:

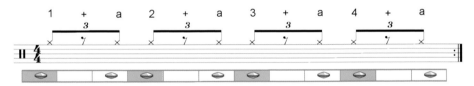

2: While still playing the hi-hat part, play a bass drum note on every count of "1" and every count of "3." This means that the hi-hat and bass drum will be played together on beats "1" and "3."

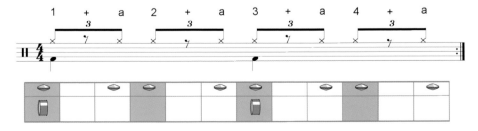

3: Next, while still playing the hi-hat and bass drum, play a snare drum note with the left hand on every count of "2" and "4."

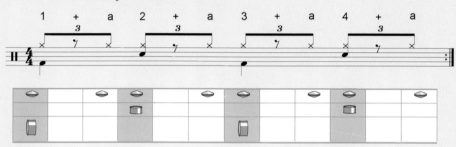

Congratulations—you are now playing a shuffle. Now continue by applying this process to another groove with a different bass drum pattern.

Exercise 2

1: Start with the hi-hat.

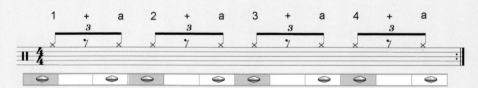

2: Next, add the bass drum. As in the previous example you will play bass drum on beats "1" and "3," but in this groove there is an additional bass drum on the "a" of "3."

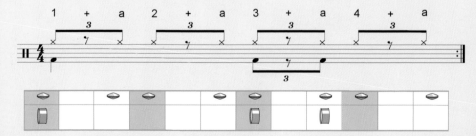

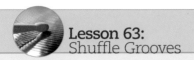

Lesson 63:
Shuffle Grooves

3: Finally, play the snare drum on "2" and "4," which completes the groove.

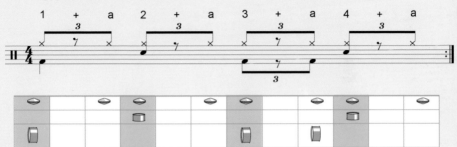

Apply this process to the following grooves.

Exercise 3

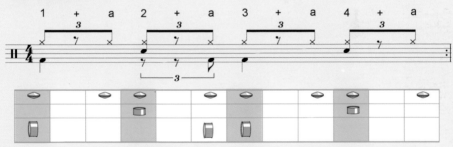

Exercise 4

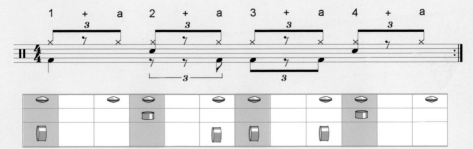

Lesson 63:
Shuffle Grooves

Exercise 5

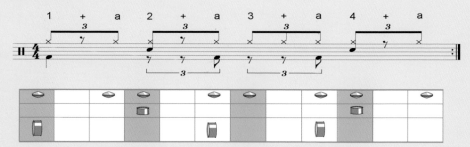

In the following exercises, only the musical notation and the count are provided.

Exercise 6

Exercise 7

Shuffle Grooves with 64
Snare Drum Variations

In the previous lesson you began developing your ability to play shuffles by playing different bass drum figures against a constant hi-hat and snare drum pattern. In this lesson, you will continue developing these grooves, this time by playing different figures on the snare drum.

The following exercises feature the same bass drum patterns as those in the previous lesson, however, an extra snare drum is added on the "a"of "4." Consequently, the hi-hat and snare drum part looks like this:

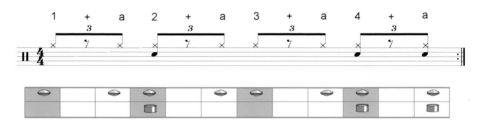

Work slowly and don't forget to count aloud. Make sure that you are comfortable playing the hi-hat and snare drum part before moving on, and remember that many of the exercises in this lesson can be heard on the audio CD.

Exercise 1 track 68

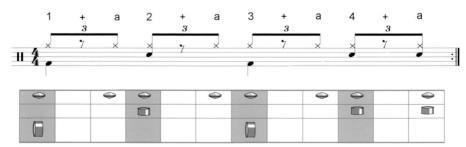

Exercise 2

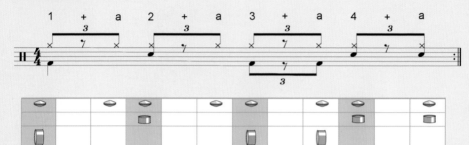

Exercise 3

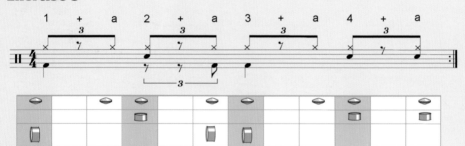

Exercise 4

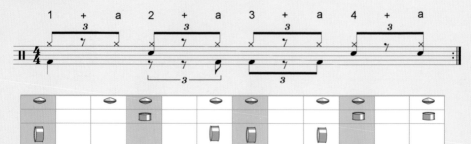

Lesson 64:
Shuffle Grooves with Snare Drum Variations

Exercise 5

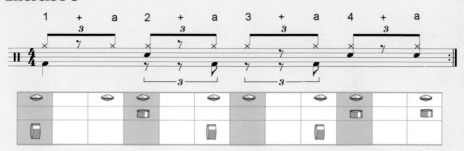

In the following exercises, you are no longer playing an extra snare drum note on the "a" of "4" but instead on the "+" of "3." The hi-hat and snare drum part is written below. Notice that the extra snare drum note falls in between the hi-hats.

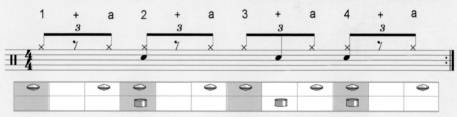

This hi-hat and snare drum pattern is the basis for the following grooves.

Exercise 6

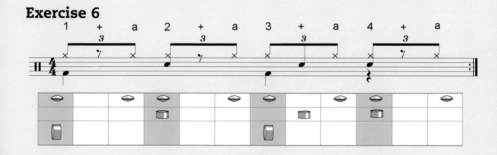

Exercise 7

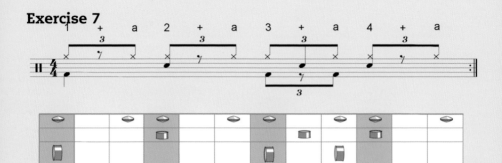

Exercise 8

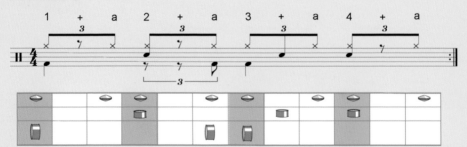

Exercise 9

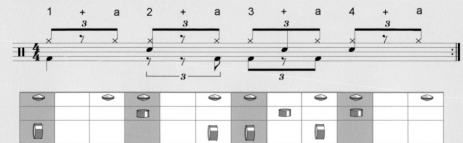

Lesson 64:
Shuffle Grooves with Snare Drum Variations

In the following exercises, both of the previous ideas are combined so that you are playing extra snare drum notes on the "+" of "1" and the "+" of "4." Also note that only the musical notation is provided.

Exercise 11

Exercise 12

Exercise 13

Exercise 14

Exercise 15

65 *Halftime Shuffle Grooves*

On the CD
Track 69

Want to read music?
See Reading and
Notation page 38.

Another type of shuffle commonly heard is the halftime shuffle.

In this case the bass drum is no longer played on "1" and "3." Nor is the snare drum played on beats "2" and "4." Instead, the bass drum is only played on beat "1" and the snare drum is played on beat "3." As the space between the bass drum and snare drum notes is now twice as big, this creates the groove's characteristic halftime feel.

Exercise 1 track 69

1: Sitting at the drums with the sticks in your hands, start by slowly counting "1 + a 2 + a 3 + a 4 + a" out aloud, over and over, making sure the counts are even. When you are comfortable with this, with the right hand play a single hi-hat note on every count of "1," "2," "3," and "4," and every "a."

The hi-hat part that you are now playing is the basis of all shuffle grooves.

Written out, it looks like this:

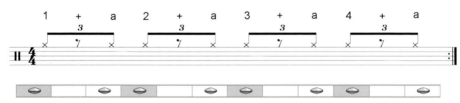

2: While still playing the hi-hat part, play a bass drum note on every count of "1."

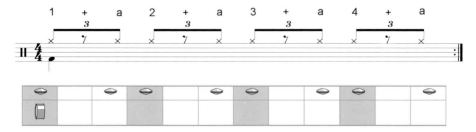

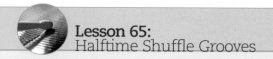

Lesson 65:
Halftime Shuffle Grooves

3: While still playing the hi-hat and bass drum, play a snare drum note with the left hand on every count of "3."

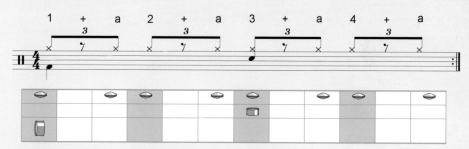

You are now playing a halftime shuffle. Now continue by applying this process to another groove with a different bass drum pattern.

Exercise 2

1: Start with the hi-hat.

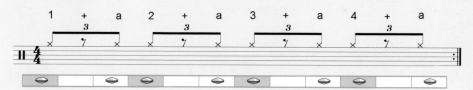

2: Add the bass drum. In this example you will play bass drum on beats "1" and "2."

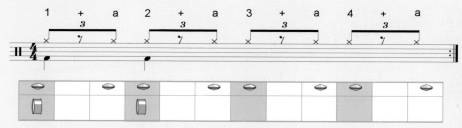

3: Playing the snare drum on "3" completes the groove.

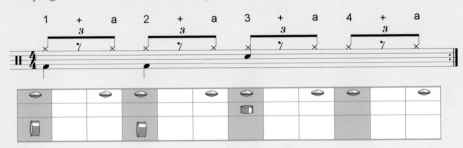

Apply this process to the following grooves.

Exercise 3

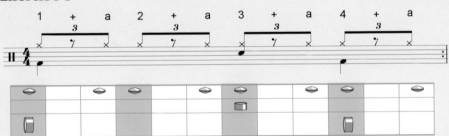

Exercise 4

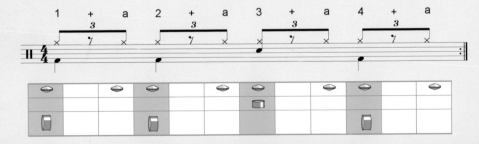

Lesson 65:
Halftime Shuffle Grooves

Exercise 5

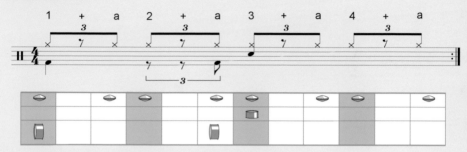

Exercise 6

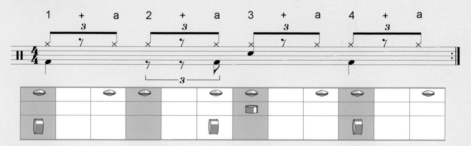

Exercise 7

Exercise 8

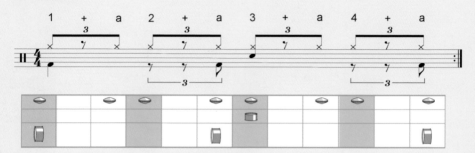

Exercise 9

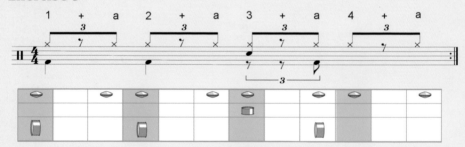

Exercise 10

Lesson 65:
Halftime Shuffle Grooves

In the following exercises, some of the previous examples are combined to create two-bar phrases. Here, only the musical notation is provided.

Exercise 11

Exercise 12

Exercise 13

Exercise 14

Exercise 15

66 Halftime Shuffle Grooves
with Snare Drum Variations

Want to read music?
See Reading and
Notation page 38.

*In the previous lesson, you began developing
your ability to play halftime shuffles by playing
different bass drum figures against a constant hi-
hat and snare drum pattern. In this lesson, you
will continue developing these grooves, this time by
playing different figures on the snare drum.*

The following exercises feature the same bass drum patterns as those in the
previous lesson, but an extra snare drum is added on the "a" of "4." Consequently,
the hi-hat and snare drum part looks like this:

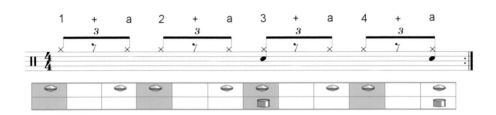

Start working very slowly, and do not forget to count aloud. Make sure that you
are comfortable playing the hi-hat and snare drum part before moving on.

Exercise 1

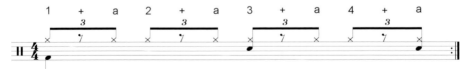

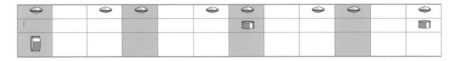

Lesson 66:
Halftime Shuffle Grooves with Snare Drum Variations

Exercise 2

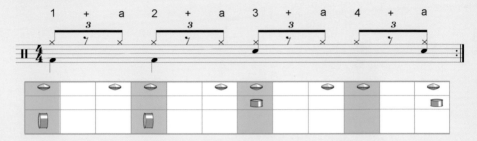

Exercise 3

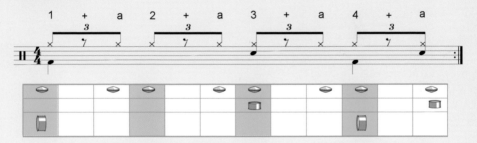

Exercise 4

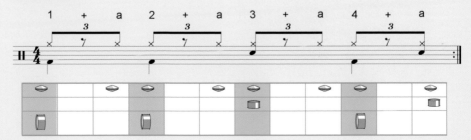

Exercise 5

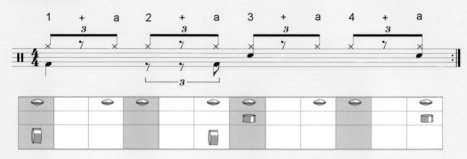

Exercise 6

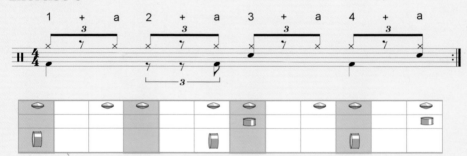

In the following exercises, you are no longer playing an extra snare drum note on the "a" of "4" but instead on the "a" of "1." The hi-hat and snare drum part is written below. Notice how this change to the snare drum part affects the groove.

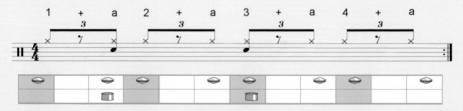

This hi-hat and snare drum pattern is the basis for the following grooves.

Lesson 66:
Halftime Shuffle Grooves with Snare Drum Variations

Exercise 7

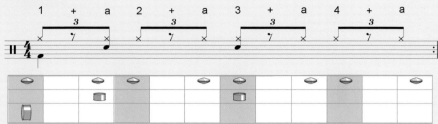

Exercise 8

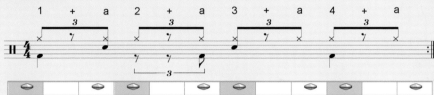

Exercise 9

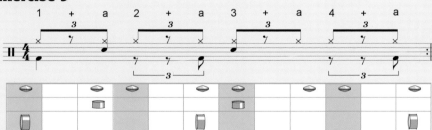

Exercise 10

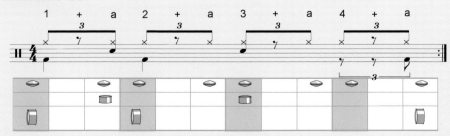

Lesson 66:
Halftime Shuffle Grooves with Snare
Drum Variations

In the following exercises, some of the previous examples are combined to create two-bar phrases. Here, only the musical notation is provided.

Exercise 11

Exercise 12

Exercise 13

Exercise 14

Exercise 15

On the CD
Tracks *70–73*

Want to read music?
See Reading and
Notation page 38.

Sixteenth-Note 67
Drum Fills

The ability to play drum fills is an
indispensable skill for any drummer.

Drum fills are used to "break up" the groove in order
to punctuate the form of the tune. For example,
drum fills might be used to create an interesting
transition between different sections of a song. Next
you will begin developing your ability to play fills
incorporating sixteenth-notes.

Exercise 1 track 70
Start with a simple two-bar phrase made up of eighth-notes played on the snare
drum with the right hand. Don't forget to count aloud.

Exercise 2 track 71
In the next example, the number of notes in the second bar is doubled to create a
bar of sixteenth-notes. Note that the right-hand continues to play eighth-notes in
both bars—the sixteenth-notes are achieved by introducing the left hand, which
plays in between the right hand. Because you are now playing sixteenth-notes,
notice how the counting system in the second bar has changed.

Lesson 67:
Sixteenth-Note Drum Fills

Exercise 3 track 72
Next, all of the eighth-notes in the first bar are moved to the closed hi-hat. The second bar remains unchanged so the right-hand will now move between hi-hat and snare drum.

Exercise 4 track 73
Add the bass drum to beats "1" and "3," and the snare drum to beats "2" and "4" of the first bar, effectively creating a groove. Again, the second bar remains unchanged.

Exercise 5
Finally, add two more bars of groove to the beginning to create a four-bar pattern. Notice that beat "1" of the first bar is now played on the crash cymbal.

On the CD
Track 74

Want to read music?
See Reading and
Notation page 38.

Sixteenth-Note 68
Drum Fills with Four
Hits Per Drum

*The following exercises will help you build your
musical vocabulary, enabling you to develop the
sixteenth-note drum fills introduced in Lesson 67.*

Remember, start very slowly and concentrate on moving around the drums as
smoothly and efficiently as possible. Get comfortable with each exercise before
increasing the tempo and refer to the audio CD where necessary.

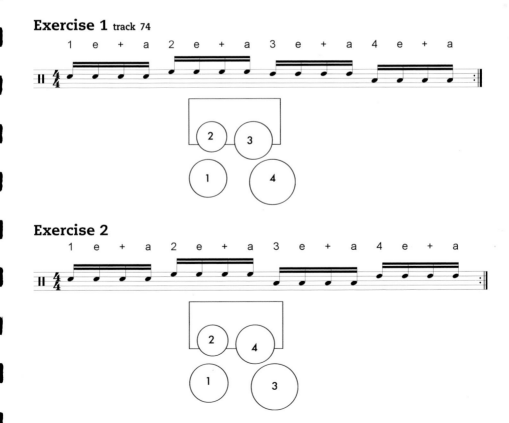

Exercise 1 track 74

Exercise 2

Exercise 3

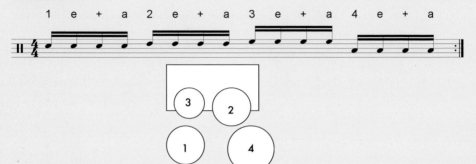

Exercise 4

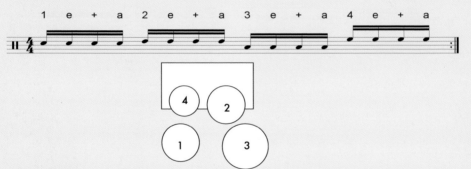

Exercise 5

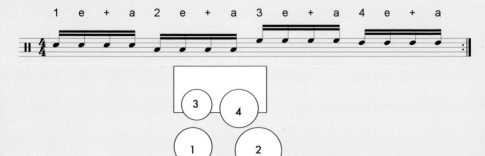

Lesson 68:
Sixteenth-Note Drum Fills with Four Hits Per Drum

Exercise 6

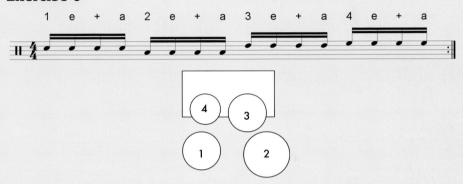

Once you are comfortable with each of these examples, it is time for you to play them in context. Do this by using each one as a drum fill, preceded by three-bars of groove, as in the previous lesson.

For example, Exercise 1 would look like this:

Notice that beat "1" of the first bar is played on the crash cymbal. Practice all of the other exercises in this chapter in the same way.

On the CD
Track 75

Want to read music?
See Reading and
Notation page 38.

69 Sixteenth-Note Drum Fills With Two Hits Per Drum

Building on the materials introduced in the previous lesson, the exercises here and over the page will help you continue to build your musical vocabulary.

In this case, each example features two-notes per drum. Remember, start very slowly and get comfortable with each exercise before increasing the tempo.

Exercise 1 track 75

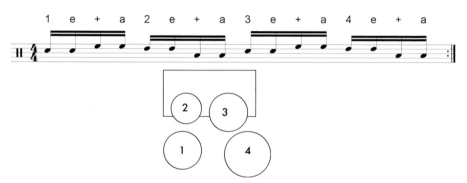

Exercise 2

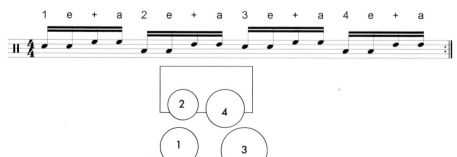

Lesson 69:
Sixteenth-Note Drum Fills with Two Hits Per Drum

Exercise 3

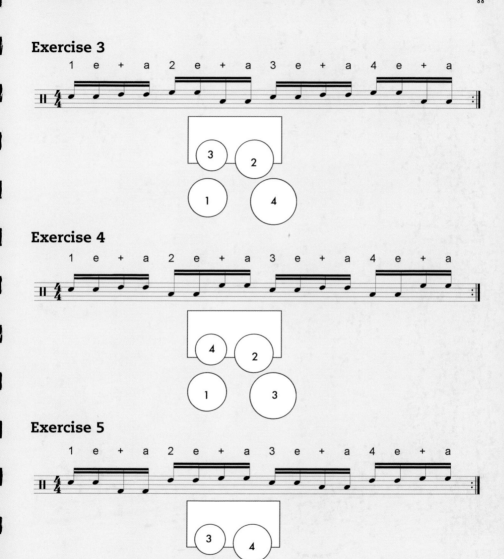

Lesson 69:
Sixteenth-Note Drum Fills With Two Hits Per Drum

Exercise 6

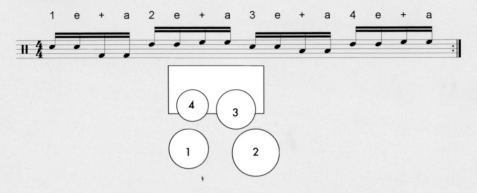

As with the previous lesson, once you are comfortable with each of these examples, it is time for you to play them in context. In this case, Exercise 1 would look like this:

Once you are comfortable with this exercise, try it using some of the other grooves that you learned in Lesson 39.

Eighth-Note Triplet Fills With Three Hits Per Drum

Having dealt with exercises involving two and four notes per drum, it is now time to look at exercises involving three hits per drums. In this case all of the exercises are triplet based—if you are unfamiliar with this concept, a full explanation is given in Lesson 10.

Because you are now playing an odd number of notes on each drum, the movements involved in these exercises can be a little tricky at first, so remember, start very slowly and concentrate on moving around the drums smoothly and efficiently.

Exercise 1 track 76

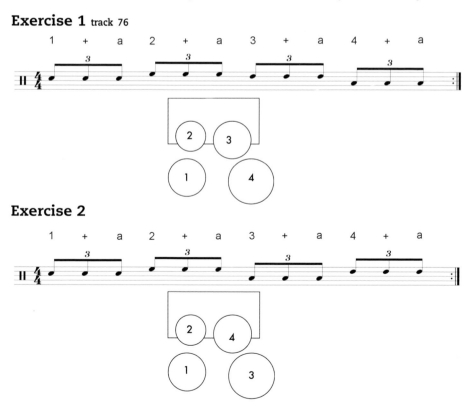

Exercise 2

Exercise 3

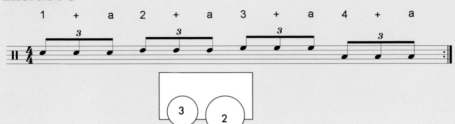

Exercise 4

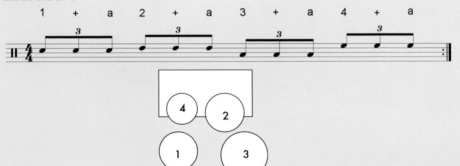

Exercise 5

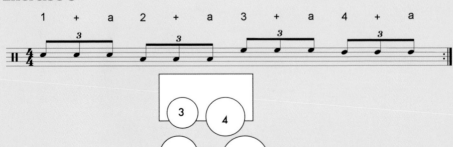

Lesson 70:
Eighth-Note Triplet Fills With Three Hits Per Drum

Exercise 6

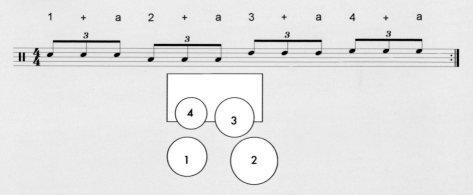

Once you are comfortable with each of these examples, it is time for you to play them in context. Do this by using each one as a drum fill, preceded by three-bars of groove, as in the previous lessons. As you are using triplets to play the fills, notice that the groove is also triplet-based.

For example, Exercise 1 would look like this:

Notice that beat "1" of the first bar is played on the crash cymbal. Practice all of the other exercises in this chapter in the same way.

71 Sixteenth-Note Fills with Tom Orchestrations

On the CD
Tracks *77–80*

Want to read music?
See Reading and
Notation page 38.

*So far, when playing these types of patterns,
both hands have moved in the same direction.
In this lesson, you will look at another way of
orchestrating sixteenth-notes around the drums,
which involves a different type of movement.*

All of the following exercises comprise a single bar of sixteenth-notes in 4/4 played with single-strokes. Based on the snare drum, each of the four sixteenth-notes in each beat is systematically moved around the toms according to a simple rule: any right-hand notes that are moved must go to the floor tom; and any left-hand notes that are moved must go to the high tom.

Therefore, in Exercise 1, the first sixteenth-note of the beat is moved to the floor tom, because this note falls on a right hand. In Exercise 2, the second sixteenth-note of the beat is moved to the high tom, because this note falls on a left hand.

Exercise 1 track 77

R   L   R   L

Exercise 2 track 78

R   L   R   L

Exercise 3 track 79

R   L   R   L

Lesson 71:
Sixteenth-Note Fills with Tom Orchestrations

Exercise 4 track 80

R   L   R   L

Exercise 5

R   L   R   L

Exercise 6

R   L   R   L

Exercise 7

R   L   R   L

Exercise 8

R   L   R   L

Lesson 71:
Sixteenth-Note Fills with Tom Orchestrations

Exercise 9

R   L   R   L

Exercise 10

R   L   R   L

Once you are comfortable with each of these examples, it is time for you to play them in context. Do this by using each one as a drum fill, preceded by three bars of groove as in the previous lessons.

For example, Exercise 1 would look like this:

Note that beat "1" of the first bar is played on the crash cymbal. Practice all of the other exercises in this chapter in the same way.

On the CD
Track 81

Want to read music?
See Reading and
Notation page 38.

One-Bar Fills 72

*Having worked through the previous exercises,
you should now be comfortable orchestrating your
sixteenth-note fills in this way.*

In this lesson the concept will be taken even farther, as you
create fills that combine the different exercises from the
previous lesson.

As an example, you will use the following patterns from the
previous lesson.

Exercise 1

R L R L

Exercise 2

R L R L

For now, let us refer to the pattern in Exercise 1 as "A" and the pattern in Exercise
2 as "B." In Exercise 3, you will see that these two patterns have been combined in
a specific way to create a new pattern

Exercise 3 track 81

R L R L

A   B   A   B

The movements involved in executing these types of patterns can be a little
tricky at first, so work slowly and deliberately. Once you are comfortable with
Exercise 3, try the following exercises.

Exercise 4

Exercise 5

Once you are comfortable with each of these examples, it is time for you to play them in context. Do this by using each one as a drum fill, preceded by three bars of groove as in the previous lessons.

For example, Exercise 3 would look like this:

Notice that beat "1" of the first bar is played on the crash cymbal. Practice all of the other exercises in this chapter in the same way. The next step is to consider fills of shorter lengths. In the following exercises, each fill is two beats long and comes on beats three and four.

Lesson 72:
One-Bar Fills

Exercise 6

Once you are comfortable playing the pattern in Exercise 6, try the following exercises.

Exercise 7

Exercise 8

Continue to experiment with similar ideas of your own.

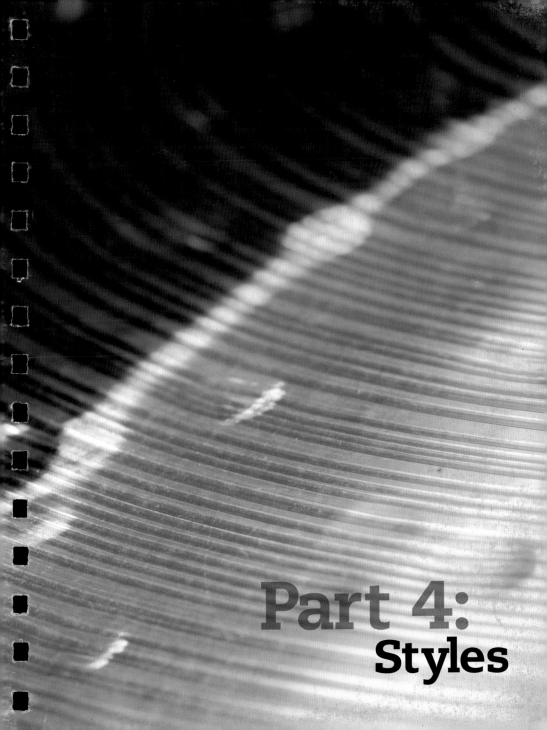

Part 4:
Styles

73 Rock

The story of rock music begins in the 1950s, when explorations in Country and Blues music led to the birth of Rock 'n' Roll. Since then it has evolved into a global phenomena, creating a plethora of sub-genres along the way, and has given rise to some of the greatest drummers of all time.

Five influential rock drummers

There have been many wonderful drummers who have contributed to the art of Rock drumming over the years, and it is, of course, impossible to document all of their achievements in this chapter. However, as a starting point I would suggest listening to the following musicians.

Led Zeppelin's John Bonham.

John Bonham: The drummer with the seminal Rock band Led Zeppelin, John Bonham defined Rock drumming for a generation of drummers. From the release of their self-titled debut album in 1969 to his untimely death in 1980, John Bonham laid down some of the most original and influential drum tracks ever. "Moby Dick," "Rock and Roll," and "Immigrant Song" are just some great examples.

Keith Moon: Drummer with The Who, Keith Moon came to epitomize the image of the Rock drummer. Known as much for his offstage antics as his playing, Keith's explosive style provided inspiration for drummers everywhere. "Substitute," "Won't Get Fooled Again," and "Baba O'Riley" are great examples.

Ringo Starr: Drummer with The Beatles, Ringo is undoubtedly one of the most influential drummers in history. Known for his highly creative and often idiosyncratic drum parts, his playing has often been misguidedly derided for its simplicity. Ringo is responsible for some of the most instantly and widely recognizable drum tracks in history. "Come Together," "A Day In The Life," and "Ticket To Ride" are great examples.

Ginger Baker: Coming to fame with The Graham Bond Organization in the 1960s, Ginger Baker is best known for his work with Eric Clapton and Jack Bruce in the band Cream. Characterized by inventive fills and use of double bass drums, his playing helped redefine Rock drumming. "Toad," "Strange Brew," and "Sunshine Of Your Love" are great examples.

Stewart Copeland: Best known for his drumming with The Police, Stewart Copeland's playing incorporated elements of Reggae, Ska, and Punk to create a highly original and much imitated style. "Message In A Bottle," "Roxanne," and "Don't Stand So Close To Me" are great examples.

Cream's Ginger Baker.

Rock grooves

Example 1: Rock 'n' Roll

Example 2: Classic Rock

Example 3: Metal

74 Blues

Blues is the music that evolved out of African-American spirituals and worksongs of the late nineteenth century.

With the birth of the Chicago Blues style in the late 1940s, the music began to incorporate electric instruments and drumsets. The explorations of early Blues drummers such as Fred Below and Francis Clay laid the foundations for what would eventually evolve into modern rock drumming.

Robben Ford's Tom Brechtlein.

Blues grooves
Below are some classic Blues grooves that every drummer should know.

Example 1: Chicago Shuffle
Although the Chicago Shuffle is one of the simplest shuffle grooves, making it feel right can be very challenging. Traditionally played on the ride with the hi-hat on beats "2" and "4," the bass drum is played on beats "1" and "3," giving it its characteristic "two feel."

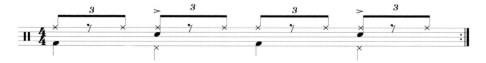

Lesson 74
Blues

Example 2: Texas Shuffle

The Texas Shuffle can be a challenging groove to play well. Traditionally played on the ride with the hi-hat on beats "2" and "4," the bass drum is played on all four beats. However, the snare drum is played in unison with the ride. The technical challenge here is to accent the snare drum on beats "2" and "4," so creating a solid backbeat while keeping the other snare drum notes quiet.

Example 3: Slow Blues 1

As the name suggests, this groove works well at slower tempos. In this groove all three parts of the triplet are played on the hi-hat and the backbeat is played on beats "2" and "4." Although the bass drum pattern here is typical, be sure to experiment with different patterns of your own.

Example 4: Slow Blues 2

Although similar to the previous example, in this case some of the hi-hat notes are subdivided, creating a little more rhythmic momentum. As well as experimenting with different bass drum patterns, try subdividing different hi-hat notes too.

75 *Funk*

Funk is the style of music that evolved in the late 1960s and early 1970s from the musical explorations of artists such as James Brown and Sly Stone.

Characterized by highly syncopated, sixteenth-note rhythms and simple forms, often based on just a couple of riffs, it is the drumbeat that lies at the heart of Funk music.

Funk drummers you should know

James Brown's Clyde Stubblefield.

Clyde Stubblefield: Another drummer best known for his work with James Brown. During the six years he spent with Brown he was responsible for some of the most memorable funk grooves ever. "Cold Sweat," "Mother Popcorn," and "Funky Drummer" are great examples.

John "Jabo" Starks: Best known as the drummer with James Brown from 1970 and 1975, during which time he played on such classics as "Super Bad," "Soul Power," and "Get Up (I Feel Like Being A) Sex Machine."

Dave Garibaldi: Drummer with San Francisco's Tower of Power, a mighty eleven-piece band that created some of the most advanced funk music of the era. Dave's innovative and sophisticated style can be heard on tracks such as "The Oakland Stroke," "Squib Cakes," and "Soul Vaccination."

Mike Clark: Mike did his most influential playing with the band Head Hunters, which featured Herbie Hancock on keyboards. His breakthrough style was best captured on the track, "Actual Proof."

Lesson 75
Funk

Zigaboo Modeliste:
Probably the most well
known exponent of
New Orleans-style funk
drumming, Zigaboo was
drummer with The Meters.
Check out his funky, broken
style on tracks such as
"Cissy Strut," "Here Comes
The Meter Man," and "Look-
Ka Py Py."

The Meter's Joseph "Zigaboo" Modeliste.

Funk grooves

Example 1

Example 2

Example 3

Example 4

76 Jazz

Since its genesis at the end of the nineteenth century, Jazz has continued to evolve, producing a diversity of connected styles.

Each musical genre has been accompanied by its own characteristic drumming style, but the history of jazz has given rise to some of the greatest and most artistic drummers ever.

Jazz drummers you should know

Jazz Legend Max Roach.

Max Roach: One of the seminal drummers of the bop era, creating new musical forms alongside contemporaries, such as Dizzy Gillespie, Charlie Parker, and Clifford Brown. Characterized by an ability to swing effortlessly at breakneck tempos, the use of form and melody in his solos, as well as the imaginative use of foot ostinatos, have contributed to Max's legendary status.

Tony Williams: Along with Elvin Jones, Tony Williams led a revolution in drumming in the 1960s that, whilst deeply connected to its antecedents, saw the dissolution of metric boundaries and a movement away from the rudiment-based vocabulary of the era to a new way of playing that ultimately became the prototype of the modern American style.

Jack DeJohnette: The archetype of the modern Jazz drummer, Jack DeJohnette succeeded in taking the innovations of his predecessors and formulating them into a highly original style characterized by sophisticated harmonic coordination. Rather than relying on the ride cymbal alone, this style shares responsibility of timekeeping between all four limbs.

Baby Dodds: One of the great drummers of the New Orleans style, Baby Dodds is best known for his work with Louis Armstrong in the early 1900s. Today he remains one of the most influential drummers ever, inspiring generations of musicians who came after him.

Gene Krupa: The most famous drummer from Chicago, Gene Krupa is largely responsible for elevating the role of the drummer from timekeeper to showman. During his time with Benny Goodman, his drum solos, such as on the classic "Sing! Sing! Sing!" became a feature.

Giant of the swing era, Gene Krupa.

Jazz grooves

Example 1

Example 2

Example 3

This pattern is an example of a style of drumming originating in New Orleans and called Second Line Drumming.

77 Latin

The term Latin is used to describe all music originating in the countries of Latin America.

This encompasses an incredible diversity of musical styles, but for drums, the rhythms of the Brazilian and Afro Cuban traditions are most popular.

Brazilian drummer Airto Moreira.

Cuban drummer Horacio "El Negro" Hernandez.

Very few of these grooves originated on the drumset, but they have become an indispensable part of its musical vocabulary. Below are some of the most common Latin grooves played on drumset today.

Afro cuban grooves

Example 1: Cascara and Clave

Example 2: Mozambique

Lesson 77
Latin

Example 3: Songo

Example 4: Guaganco

Example 5: Afro Cuban 6/8

Brazilian grooves

Example 1: Samba

Example 2: Bossa Nova

78 Electronica

Increasingly, dance music with its impossibly layered beats and sonic diversity, is becoming a source of inspiration for acoustic drummers who seek to emulate the programed and processed grooves of the different electronic styles.

Over the last few years these programed beats have migrated to a diversity of other styles of music including Jazz and Pop, and consequently a working knowledge of dance music is becoming more and more important to drumset players.

Jojo Mayer is one of the most innotative drummers to have explored electronic music.

Example 1: Drum 'n' Bass

Example 2: House

Example 3: Techno

Country 79

Becoming prominent in the 1920s, Country music developed out of American Southern Folk music. Along with Blues, Country music is responsible for the birth of Rock 'n' Roll.

Country grooves

Example 1: The Train Beat
Referred to as The Train Beat because of its driving eighth-note snare drum pattern, this groove has the bass drum on beats "1" and "3" and the hi-hat on "2" and "4." Traditionally it would be played using single-strokes but feel free to experiment with different stickings.

Buddy Harman has played on over 18,000 recording sessions and is credited with helping to create the "Nashville Sound."

Example 2: Cut Time
This groove is a straight-cut-time groove involving quarter-notes on the ride, a backbeat on beats "2" and "4," bass drum on "1" and "3," and hi-hat on "2" and "4."

80 *Hip Hop*

Developed in the early 1970s, Hip Hop is a culture that embodies a musical style founded by the DJs and MCs of Brooklyn and the Bronx in New York City.

DJs such as Kool Herc would loop the drumbreaks on old funk and R 'n' B records while MCs would freestyle poetry and lyrics over the top. Over the years these musical explorations have evolved into a global business where Rappers are megastars with their own clothing lines.

Hip Hop Pioneer Kool Herc.

Example 1

Example 2

Reggae and Caribbean Music 81

From the Calypso and Soca of Trinidad, to the Reggae and Ska of Jamaica, the music of the Caribbean encompasses a wide diversity of genres.

Often characterized by its highly infectious grooves, the music of this region presents the drummer with some interesting possibilities. The patterns that follow are examples of some of the most common Afro Caribbean rhythms played on the drumset.

Reggae and Caribbean grooves

Example 1: One Drop

Example 2: Four Drop

Example 3: Calypso

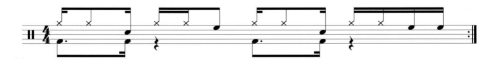

Example 4: Soca

Resources

Periodicals

Modern Drummer magazine

Modern Drummer is the world's most widely-read drumming magazine and features interviews, reviews, and educational articles.

Rhythm magazine & Drummer magazine

These two great drumming magazines are published in the UK and feature interviews, reviews, and educational articles with many of the world's top players. Rhythm magazine also comes with an educational CD, featuring play-a-long audio tracks and video demonstrations of the lessons.

Websites

justindrums.com

The author's own website, packed full of a huge range of free online drum lessons.

mikedolbear.com

One of the largest drum websites in the world, Mike's site is a great resource for drummers. It features lots of useful information such as reviews, interviews, and news about all your favorite players, as well as a popular forum where you can discuss all things drumming with players from all over the world.

drummerworld.com

A great site featuring information about all of your favorite players.

mapexdrums.com

Website for Mapex, one of the biggest and most popular drum manufacturers in the world. This site features some cool imagery as well as information about all of their products, and is a great place to start if you're looking for that new drumset.

paiste.com

Website for cymbal manufacturer, Paiste. As well as providing information about their range of products, this site features some great general information about cymbals and cymbal making.

shawstix.com

Website of drumstick company Shaw where you can see a complete range of drumsticks, as seen throughout this book.

aquariandrumheads.com

Website for Aquarian drumheads, this is the place to see all of the types of drumheads discussed earlier in the book.

Organizations

The Percussive Arts Society

A professional organization promoting information, communication, and education for the percussive community. Their website offers lots of information and advice for beginners as well as professionals.

32 E. Washington,
Suite 1400,
Inndianapolis,
IN 46204
Website: pas.org

Index

Page numbers in bold italics
refer to illustrations

Use this handy fold-out guide as
a quick reference to the symbols
and notation used in this book

Understanding the symbols and abbreviations

Key to the symbols

⬬	Closed hi-hat
⬬	Open hi-hat
◇	Ride cymbal
▭	Snare drum
▯	Bass drum

Key to the abbreviations

RH	Rght hand
LH	Left hand
R	Right
L	Left
D	Down stroke
U	Up stroke
T	Tap stroke
F	Full stroke

Understanding the musical notation
(see pages 38–63)

The notes

Note	Value
𝅝	4 beats
𝅗𝅥	2 beats
𝅘𝅥	1 beat
𝅘𝅥𝅮	1/2 beat
𝅘𝅥𝅯	1/4 beat
𝅘𝅥𝅰	1/8 beat

The rests

Note	Value
—	4 beats
—	2 beats
𝄽	1 beat
𝄾	1/2 beat
𝄿	1/4 beat
𝅀	1/8 beat

Understanding conventions (see pages 38–63)

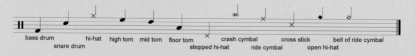

bass drum · snare drum · hi-hat · high tom · mid tom · floor tom · stepped hi-hat · crash cymbal · ride cymbal · cross stick · open hi-hat · bell of ride cymbal

Credits

Quarto would like to thank and acknowledge the following for supplying illustrations and photographs reproduced in this book.

Key: a above, b below, l left, r right.
BradleySmith/Corbis:12r DeltahazeCorporation /Redferns:13al Max Jones' File/Redferns:14ar NAMM resource center:15ar Outline Press/Redferns:18r Regal Tip: 31l,32,33 Shutterstock:34al,bl,br Boss:35al,ar HQRealfeel: 35bl Gibraltar:35b Moongel:35br Korg:35a Roland:36ar 37 HorizonInternationalImages/ Alamy:40l DavidRedfern/Redferns:40r Alan Myers/Alamy:64 IanGoodrick/Alamy:65r AndrewLepley/Redferns:81bl Globephotos/Rex features:236 bl Rex features:237a HowardDenner/ Retna: 238l Robin Little/Redferns:240bl ClaytonCall/Redferns: 241ar DavidRedfern/ Redferns: 242l BobWilloughby/Redferns: 243ar Andrew Lepley/Redferns: 244al,244ar Ebet Roberts/Redferns: 246al Rick Malkin:247ar.

Author Acknowledgements

With endless gratitude to my wonderful parents, Michael and Lynn not only for your inexhaustible support and encouragement, but also for stumping the cash that paid for my musical education and tolerating all of the noise until we discovered sound-proofing!

Also thanks to Duncan, Martin, and Pete at Mapex and Paiste; Craig at Music Shipping; Pete, Paul, and the all of the guys at the ICMP; Tom and Olly for loving drums as much as I do.

And to Jules... just for being you.